CRIMINAL JUSTICE, LAW ENFORCEMI

# OFFENDER REENTRY

# BACKGROUND, FEDERAL PROGRAMS, AND AN ANNOTATED BIBLIOGRAPHY

# CRIMINAL JUSTICE, LAW ENFORCEMENT AND CORRECTIONS

Additional books in this series can be found on Nova's website under the Series tab.

Additional e-books in this series can be found on Nova's website under the e-book tab.

CRIMINAL JUSTICE, LAW ENFORCEMENT AND CORRECTIONS

# OFFENDER REENTRY

# BACKGROUND, FEDERAL PROGRAMS, AND AN ANNOTATED BIBLIOGRAPHY

## MICAH J. HIRAM
### EDITOR

*New York*

For permission to use material from this book please contact us:
Telephone 631-231-7269; Fax 631-231-8175
Web Site: http://www.novapublishers.com

### NOTICE TO THE READER

The Publisher has taken reasonable care in the preparation of this book, but makes no expressed or implied warranty of any kind and assumes no responsibility for any errors or omissions. No liability is assumed for incidental or consequential damages in connection with or arising out of information contained in this book. The Publisher shall not be liable for any special, consequential, or exemplary damages resulting, in whole or in part, from the readers' use of, or reliance upon, this material. Any parts of this book based on government reports are so indicated and copyright is claimed for those parts to the extent applicable to compilations of such works.

Independent verification should be sought for any data, advice or recommendations contained in this book. In addition, no responsibility is assumed by the publisher for any injury and/or damage to persons or property arising from any methods, products, instructions, ideas or otherwise contained in this publication.

This publication is designed to provide accurate and authoritative information with regard to the subject matter covered herein. It is sold with the clear understanding that the Publisher is not engaged in rendering legal or any other professional services. If legal or any other expert assistance is required, the services of a competent person should be sought. FROM A DECLARATION OF PARTICIPANTS JOINTLY ADOPTED BY A COMMITTEE OF THE AMERICAN BAR ASSOCIATION AND A COMMITTEE OF PUBLISHERS.

Additional color graphics may be available in the e-book version of this book.

**Library of Congress Cataloging-in-Publication Data**

ISBN: 978-1-63117-496-4

*Published by Nova Science Publishers, Inc. † New York*

# CONTENTS

# PREFACE

This book discusses the correctional statistics, reintegration of released offenders into communities, and recidivism.

Chapter 1 - The prison population in the United States has been growing steadily for more than 30 years. The Bureau of Justice Statistics reports that since 2000 an average of 680,000 inmates have been released annually from state and federal prisons and almost 5 million ex-offenders are under some form of community-based supervision. Offender reentry can include all the activities and programming conducted to prepare ex-convicts to return safely to the community and to live as law-abiding citizens. Some ex-offenders, however, eventually end up back in prison. The most recent national-level recidivism study is 10 years old; this study showed that two-thirds of ex-offenders released in 1994 came back into contact with the criminal justice system within three years of their release. Compared with the average American, ex-offenders are less educated, less likely to be gainfully employed, and more likely to have a history of mental illness or substance abuse—all of which have been shown to be incarceration risk factors.

Three phases are associated with offender reentry programs: programs that take place during incarceration, which aim to prepare offenders for their eventual release; programs that take place during offenders' release period, which seek to connect ex-offenders with the various services they may require; and long-term programs that take place as ex-offenders permanently reintegrate into their communities, which attempt to provide offenders with support and supervision. There is a wide array of offender reentry program designs, and these programs can differ significantly in range, scope, and methodology. Researchers in the offender reentry field have suggested that the best programs begin during incarceration and extend throughout the release and reintegration process. Despite the relative lack of research in the field of offender reentry, an emerging "what works" literature suggests that programs focusing on work training and placement, drug and mental health treatment, and housing assistance have proven to be effective.

The federal government's involvement in offender reentry programs typically occurs through grant funding, which is available through a wide array of federal programs at the Departments of Justice, Labor, Education, and Health and Human Services. However, only a handful of grant programs in the federal government are designed explicitly for offender reentry purposes.

The Second Chance Act (P.L. 110-199) was enacted on April 9, 2008. The act expanded the existing offender reentry grant program at the Department of Justice and created a wide array of targeted grant-funded pilot programs.

Chapter 2 - Each year, more than 700,000 individuals are released from state and federal prisons. Another 9 million cycle through local jails. When reentry fails, the costs—both societal and economic—are high. Because reentry intersects with issues of health and housing, education and employment, family, faith, and community well-being, many federal agencies are focusing on the reentry population with initiatives that aim to improve outcomes in each of these areas. This annotated bibliography addresses issues surrounding the reentry of offenders into the community. 135 entries are organized according to: reentry websites; reentry in general; reentry by category for community corrections, jails, prisons, community and family support, employment and housing, health and safety, and special populations; and reentry skills building.

In: Offender Reentry
Editor: Micah J. Hiram

ISBN: 978-1-63117-496-4
© 2014 Nova Science Publishers, Inc.

*Chapter 1*

# OFFENDER REENTRY: CORRECTIONAL STATISTICS, REINTEGRATION INTO THE COMMUNITY, AND RECIDIVISM[*]

## *Nathan James*

## SUMMARY

The prison population in the United States has been growing steadily for more than 30 years. The Bureau of Justice Statistics reports that since 2000 an average of 680,000 inmates have been released annually from state and federal prisons and almost 5 million ex-offenders are under some form of community-based supervision. Offender reentry can include all the activities and programming conducted to prepare ex-convicts to return safely to the community and to live as law-abiding citizens. Some ex-offenders, however, eventually end up back in prison. The most recent national-level recidivism study is 10 years old; this study showed that two-thirds of ex- offenders released in 1994 came back into contact with the criminal justice system within three years of their release. Compared with the average American, ex-offenders are less educated, less likely to be gainfully employed, and more likely to have a history of mental illness or substance abuse—all of which have been shown to be incarceration risk factors.

---

[*] This is an edited, reformatted and augmented version of a Congressional Research Service Publication, CRS Report for Congress RL34287, dated June 3, 2013.

Three phases are associated with offender reentry programs: programs that take place during incarceration, which aim to prepare offenders for their eventual release; programs that take place during offenders' release period, which seek to connect ex-offenders with the various services they may require; and long-term programs that take place as ex-offenders permanently reintegrate into their communities, which attempt to provide offenders with support and supervision. There is a wide array of offender reentry program designs, and these programs can differ significantly in range, scope, and methodology. Researchers in the offender reentry field have suggested that the best programs begin during incarceration and extend throughout the release and reintegration process. Despite the relative lack of research in the field of offender reentry, an emerging "what works" literature suggests that programs focusing on work training and placement, drug and mental health treatment, and housing assistance have proven to be effective.

The federal government's involvement in offender reentry programs typically occurs through grant funding, which is available through a wide array of federal programs at the Departments of Justice, Labor, Education, and Health and Human Services. However, only a handful of grant programs in the federal government are designed explicitly for offender reentry purposes.

The Second Chance Act (P.L. 110-199) was enacted on April 9, 2008. The act expanded the existing offender reentry grant program at the Department of Justice and created a wide array of targeted grant-funded pilot programs.

## BACKGROUND

Over 95% of the prison population today will be released at some point in the future.[1] Since 2000, an average of 682,000 inmates have been released annually from state and federal prisons.[2] The Department of Justice's (DOJ's) Bureau of Justice Statistics (BJS) has estimated that two-thirds of all released prisoners will commit new offenses (recidivate) within three years of their release.[3] Many studies have indicated that reentry initiatives that combine work training and placement with counseling and housing assistance can reduce recidivism rates.[4] According to the BJS, the average per prisoner cost of incarceration in state prison in 2010 was approximately $28,000 per year.[5] States collectively spent nearly $48.5 billion on their correctional systems in 2010, the most recent year for which data are available.[6]

Offender reentry includes all the activities and programming conducted to prepare ex-convicts to return safely to the community and to live as law-abiding citizens. Reentry programs are typically divided into three phases: programs that prepare offenders to reenter society while they are in prison, programs that connect ex-offenders with services immediately after they are released from prison, and programs that provide long-term support and supervision for ex-offenders as they settle into communities permanently. Offender reentry programs vary widely in range, scope, and methodology. The best-designed programs, according to the research in the field, are those that span all three phases.[7]

A Government Accountability Office (GAO) report also suggests that post-release planning should begin as early as possible, ideally as soon as an inmate is admitted into prison or even immediately after sentencing. Such planning could include helping the offender to develop the skills and knowledge base necessary to find a job and have access to education, such as General Equivalency Degree classes for those who have not completed high school, and either vocational training or college classes for those that have completed high school but have not entered into a career.[8]

As offenders approach their release date, the research suggests that reentry planning focus on connecting offenders with the community and workplace resources they will need to get established. Again, employment and access to education have been cited by many studies as two of the most important aspects contributing to the successful reintegration of ex-offenders into society.[9] Lastly, studies suggest it is important for the reentry process to continue as offenders reintegrate into society. Indeed, for many offenders, the first few weeks of adjustment after release are actually less difficult than the longer period of community reintegration.[10] In many cases, this period of time can span the entire three to five years that offenders are sometimes supervised in the community.[11]

## CORRECTIONAL SYSTEM STATISTICS

To understand the issue of offender reentry, one must first understand the ways in which ex-offenders are released into the community. It is also worthwhile to analyze the population of individuals serving sentences in correctional facilities, because the number of offenders re-entering the community is necessarily related to the number and type of offenders serving prison sentences. This section analyzes national data on the nation's correctional system.

## Population in Correctional Facilities

The correctional system includes two main forms of detention: jails and prisons. Jails, also known as local lockups, are facilities generally used to temporarily detain individuals who have been arrested or charged with a crime but not usually convicted.[12] The jail population is thus extremely fluid, with individuals usually staying for a matter of weeks, and includes individuals who may never be convicted of a crime. Prisons, on the other hand, typically house individuals who have been convicted of a crime and sentenced to a term of one year or longer. For this reason, the prison population is less fluid than the jail population.

The number of inmates incarcerated in correctional facilities steadily increased between 1980 and 2008 when it reached its peak of just more than 2.3 million inmates. However, in recent years the number of incarcerated individuals has declined. The number of inmates in state prisons and local jails decreased by 15,400 (-0.7%) inmates in 2009, 21,900 (-1.0%) inmates in 2010, and 30,400 (-1.3%) inmates in 2011. The decrease in the correctional population in 2009 was the result of a declining jail population, but in 2010 and 2011, there was a decrease in the number of inmates held in both jails and prisons. Between 1980 and 2008, the number of people imprisoned in the United States increased, on average, 5.7% per year. However, the number of incarcerated persons has decreased, on average, by 1.0% annually since 2009. **Figure 1** shows the annual population in state and federal correctional facilities from 1980 to 2011 (the most recent data available).

Given the fact that 95% of all inmates will eventually return to the community,[13] the prison population has a direct impact on offender reentry. As the prison population grows, increasing numbers of ex-offenders are being released from correctional facilities. Most of these ex- offenders are required to undergo some form of community supervision as part of their release. The following section explores the mechanisms and statistics surrounding the release of prisoners into the community.

## Offenders under Community Supervision

Ex-offenders can be released into the community through a variety of different mechanisms. Some offenders never serve prison sentences and instead serve their sentence on probation in their communities under supervision. Others serve most of their sentences in correctional facilities but are then released on parole to finish their sentences in their communities under supervision. Lastly, some offenders serve out their entire sentences in correctional facilities and are released unconditionally into the community.

## *Probation*

Individuals who are found guilty of committing a crime that is deemed not serious enough for imprisonment can be sentenced to serve their sentences under community supervision (probation). Offenders on probation typically must adhere to certain conditions and check in regularly with their probation officers. Violation of these conditions or failure to appear before their probation officers can lead to further criminal sanctions, including incarceration. In some instances, offenders can be sentenced to a mixed term of prison and probation.

## *Parole*

Individuals who have served most of their sentences in a correctional facility are sometimes eligible to complete their sentences in the community under conditional supervision. While some states have a parole system in place, Congress abolished parole at the federal level effective in 1986. However, there is a small percentage of federal offenders who were sentenced prior to 1986 who are still eligible for parole. The conditions associated with parole can vary from case to case, but typically include drug testing and regular contact with a parole officer. Violations of these conditions can result in the parolee returning to prison to serve out the remaining portion of his or her sentence. There are two different kinds of parole: discretionary and mandatory.

## Discretionary Parole

States that use parole boards to determine whether a prisoner should be released into the community have discretionary parole. Parole boards have the authority to conditionally release a prisoner into the community based on a statutory or an administrative determination that the prisoner is eligible.

## Mandatory Parole

States that have statutory language determining when offenders should be released into the community have mandatory parole. Jurisdictions that use determinate sentencing[14] often include provisions specifying when inmates should be conditionally released from prison after serving a specified portion of their original sentences.

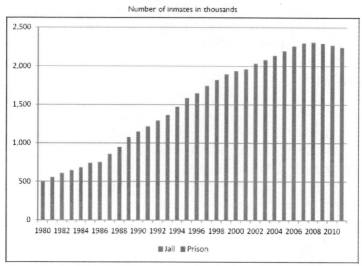

Number of inmates in thousands

Source: *Sourcebook of Criminal Justice Statistics (online)*, Table 6.1.2011.

Figure 1. Number of Inmates Incarcerated in the United States, 1980-2011.

**Figure 2** shows the number of offenders who were supervised in the community, either through probation or through parole, during the period from 1980 to 2011. It is important to note that between 1980 and 2011, parolees accounted for, on average, 16% of the overall population under community supervision. The growing state prison population has resulted in a concomitant growth in the overall population of offenders under community supervision. Interestingly, however, the growth rate of individuals under community supervision has been lagging behind the growth rate of individuals in correctional facilities. This is likely due to the fact that a growing number of offenders are being released directly into the community without any form of supervision. **Figure 2** shows that the number of offenders under community supervision increased by approximately 260% from 1980 to 2011; this contrasts with the overall prison population, which grew by approximately 346% during this period.

The relationship between the prison and parole populations is an important one for a number of reasons. Offenders serving their sentences in prison have generally committed more serious crimes than offenders who serve their sentences in jail or on probation; as previously noted, the prison population typically includes individuals sentenced to more than a year of incarceration. Parolees, meanwhile, often return to the community after a prolonged period of incarceration and usually face a period of adjustment.

Number of offenders in millions

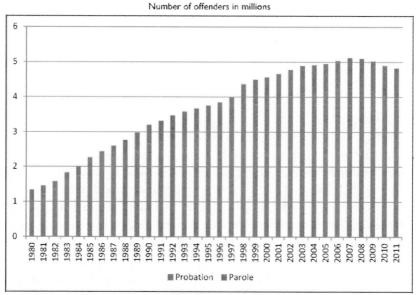

Source: *Sourcebook of Criminal Justice Statistics (online)*, Table 6.1.2011.

Figure 2. Number of Offenders Under Community Supervision, 1980-2011.

**Figure 3** shows the relationship between annual changes in the prison and the parole populations. **Figure 3** shows a differentiation between the period from 1983 to 1992, when the annual increase in the parole population generally outstripped the annual increase in the prison population, and the period from 1993 to 2006, when the obverse has largely been true. This is interesting for a number of reasons. The population of offenders on parole is, by definition, a subset of the population of offenders in prison: to get parole, one has to pass through the prison system. The fact that, in general, the population in prison has been increasing at a faster rate than the population on parole over the past 18 years suggests that fewer prisoners are being released before the end of their sentences; this corresponds with the sentencing reform efforts implemented by many states in the 1980s and early 1990s and the growing use of truth-in-sentencing laws by states. Truth-in-sentencing laws require that offenders serve a substantial portion of their sentences (usually three-quarters), thereby reducing discrepancies between the sentence imposed and the actual time served in prison.[15] Additionally, the discrepancy between the annual growth of the parole and prison populations in the 1990s is also a result of the fact that prison sentences have become longer because of the enactment of mandatory minimum sentencing laws by most states. Taken together, these factors could suggest that the parole population may begin to grow faster than the prison population in coming years as the longer sentences that have been issued over the past two decades come closer to being completed.

## Recidivism

Recidivism is often defined as the rearrest, reconviction, or reincarceration of an ex-offender within a given time frame. As a result of this broad definition of recidivism, most studies include technical violations of an offender's parole or probation (such as failing a drug test or not showing up for a meeting, for example) within their general recidivism statistics. Rearrest statistics also include individuals who are found innocent of the charges. For these reasons, some studies have focused on reincarceration with a new prison sentence as a more accurate recidivism statistic, arguing that technical violations are really an extension of an offender's original prison term and not a newly committed crime. Essentially, there are two competing philosophies about what recidivism should mean.[16] On the one hand are those who argue that any new contact with the criminal justice system, no matter how minor, should be considered recidivism on the part of an ex-offender.[17] On the other hand are those who argue that recidivism should be more narrowly defined as the commission of a new crime, resulting in a new sentence, by an ex-offender.[18] What one includes in the definition of recidivism has a substantial impact on the rate of recidivism reported.

Regardless of what definition is used, recidivism is a difficult subject to study. Tracking recidivism involves following the cases of individuals for a number of years and relying on state or national-level data sets that contain inherent inaccuracies. For example, if an offender is released in California but commits a new crime in Maine, the researchers must be able to match those two records together to make a definitive statement about recidivism. This match is typically done by consulting the FBI's master database of convictions; however, as we will see later, this database contains omissions that may affect the results of recidivism studies. A number of studies have been conducted on this issue, and most states have calculated their own recidivism rates. However, there is a dearth of current national-level statistics on recidivism by ex-offenders. The two main national-level studies that have been conducted over the last 15 years are outlined below.

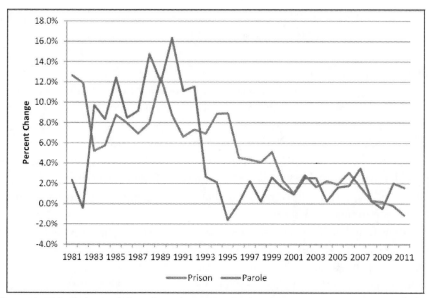

Source: *CRS analysis of data from Sourcebook of Criminal Justice Statistics (online)*,
Table 6.1.2011.

Figure 3. Annual Change in the Prison and Parole Population.

## Bureau of Justice Statistics 1994 Recidivism Study

One of the most comprehensive national-level recidivism study to date was conducted by the Bureau of Justice Statistics (BJS) and dates back to 1994.[19] The BJS study examined the rearrest, reconviction, and reincarceration of prisoners from 15 states three years after their release in 1994.[20] The study tracked 272,111 prisoners, or almost two-thirds of all the prisoners released from state prisons in 1994.

After three years, the study found that over two-thirds (67.5%) of the prisoners released had been rearrested for a new offense. Almost half (46.9%) of the prisoners had been reconvicted of a new crime. Just over half (51.8%) of the prisoners released were back in prison either because they had been resentenced to prison for a new crime they had committed (25.4%) or because they had violated some technical provision of their release (26.4%).[21] The BJS study therefore showed that more than half of ex-offenders who return to prison do so because of technical violations of their parole or probation rather than the commission of a new crime. It is important to note that the BJS study did not include information on what percentage of ex-offenders were serving time in local jails; however, as previously noted, local jails feature a fluid population of inmates who usually reside there for a brief period of time and may not be convicted of the crime for which they are being held.

### Pew Recidivism Study

The Pew Center on the States (Pew), in collaboration with the Association of State Correctional Administrators (ASCA), surveyed each state's department of corrections in an attempt to collect a single source of state-by-state recidivism data.[22] The survey asked states to provide 36-month recidivism rates for offenders released in 1999 and 2004.[23] Thirty-three states provided data for the 1999 release cohort and 41 states provided data for the 2004 release cohort. Pew reported that the data allowed them to analyze recidivism trends in 33 states.

Pew found that, when only considering the states that reported data on both cohorts, the recidivism rate for inmates released in 1999 was 45.4%, and for inmates released in 2004 it was 43.3%. The recidivism rate decreased slightly between 1999 and 2004 even though nearly 64,000 more inmates were released in 2004 than in 1999. Of the offenders in the 1999 cohort, 19.9% of them were reincarcerated for a new crime, while 25.5% were returned to prison for a technical violation of post-incarceration supervision. Of the offenders in the 2004 cohort, 22.3% of them were reincarcerated for a new crime, while 21% were returned to prison for a technical violation of post-incarceration supervision. Pew also compared reported recidivism rates for inmates released in 1999 and 2004 from the 15 states included in the 1994 BJS recidivism study (see above) and found that recidivism rates have remained relatively stable over time. The 1999 and 2004 recidivism rates for the states included in the 1994 BJS study (excluding California) were 39.7% and 38.5%, respectively, which is similar to the 40.1% recidivism rate calculated by BJS (if California is excluded).[24]

### United States Sentencing Commission Study

The United States Sentencing Commission (USSC) studied the recidivism rates of a random sample of 6,062 offenders who were sentenced under federal sentencing guidelines in FY1992. The recidivism information was derived from the "RAP" sheet criminal history repository maintained by the FBI's Criminal Justice Information Services Division, which has certain limitations (discussed below). The USSC study examined the relationship between the offenders' sentences and recidivism rates. The USSC developed the Criminal History Category (CHC) based on a review of prediction measures that were popularized in a National Academy of Sciences study in the 1980s.[25]

Generally, an offender's prior criminal record will determine which CHC they are placed in. There are six CHC levels; an offender's placement within these levels is determined by a points system based on their prior contacts with the criminal justice system.

Points are awarded for prior convictions, for violations of technical provisions of their judicial supervision (e.g., bail or parole), and for violent crimes. Juvenile and special court martial convictions are also counted. The higher the CHC, the more severe the offender's criminal history is.[26]

Generally, the study showed that an offender's criminal history was strongly associated with the likelihood of the offender recidivating after being released. The more prior convictions or the more serious the nature of the offender's crimes, the more likely the offender was to recidivate. The study also showed that the definition of recidivism had a large impact on the resulting statistics. For example, for the most hardened ex-offenders, general recidivism, which includes any contact with the criminal justice system, was at 55% after two years. Over this same period, the re-conviction rate for the most hardened ex-offenders was only 15%. This discrepancy shows that the definition of recidivism is important; even for the most hardened ex-offenders, the reconviction rate was relatively low compared with the general recidivism.

### National Recidivism Study Limitations

The data used in the BJS, Pew and USSC studies come from official records maintained by the states' and the Federal Bureau of Investigation's (FBI's) official criminal history repositories. These repositories understate the actual recidivism levels to some unknown extent because they rely on local police agencies and courts to supply them with notifying documents. These documents are not always filed by local police departments or courts, however. In addition, if the offender provided a different name or a fraudulent identity document to police, and this misinformation was not discovered, they would likely not be captured by the data. Lastly, even if the criminal is correctly identified and the document is sent to the repository, the repository may not be able to match the person identified in the document with their records. This could occur, for example, if the document that has been submitted is filled out incorrectly or is illegible.

Moreover, as previously noted, there is some debate about what kind of outcome measure should be included when measuring recidivism. Should recidivism statistics include any contact with the criminal justice system by an ex-offender? Or should recidivism statistics be limited to the commission of crimes by ex-offenders that result in new convictions or new sentences? Both the BJS and the USSC studies showed wide differentials between general recidivism, which includes any contact with the criminal justice system, and re-conviction rates for new crimes. The length of the follow-up period will also play a role in the recidivism statistics that are generated. Because of the costs and difficulties associated with studying recidivism, most studies follow ex- offenders for two or three years. There is a dearth of information concerning what happens to ex- offenders beyond the three-year window that is typically studied.

For all of these reasons, caution should be taken when attempting to draw conclusions about the efficacy of policy measures based solely on recidivism statistics. When using recidivism statistics to evaluate a program, it is important to understand exactly what is included in the definition of recidivism. For example, consider the following hypothetical scenario: a program is evaluated and shows significant decreases in the number of ex-offenders that are convicted of new crimes and sentenced to new prison terms; however, the number of ex-offenders arrested for violating their parole actually increased. Was this program successful or not? Did it make society safer or not? This may well be an unlikely scenario, but it calls attention to the fact that recidivism may mean different things to different people. While recidivism statistics remain the best information available concerning whether ex-offenders come into contact with the criminal justice system after being released from prison and what the nature of that contact is, they are but one factor to be considered when evaluating the efficacy of a program, because of the concerns outlined above.

### *Importance of Considering Other Outcome Measures*

While recidivism has traditionally been the most widely used metric used to determine the effectiveness of correctional and reentry programs, it is important to note here that other outcome measures can help determine whether an offender's reintegration into society is succeeding. Measures of attachment to social institutions, such as employment, involvement in community activities, church-going, and participation in support groups, can be important bellwethers of an offender's transition to the community.[27] For example, one study of drug court[28] participants showed that drug courts reduce drug use among their participants and that children born to drug court participants are less likely to be born addicted to drugs.[29] Given the high societal costs associated with substance-dependent infants, for that particular program, recidivism was arguably not the most important outcome measure that could have been considered. To give policy makers a better idea of what happens to ex-offenders, program evaluations are best focused on the entire universe of activities in which ex-offenders engage. A potential issue for Congress could be whether these alternate measures of an offender reentry program's effectiveness in fostering reintegration within the community should be considered when deciding how best to allocate grant funding and other government resources. A related issue could be whether reporting on these alternate outcome measures should be required of programs receiving federal grant funding.

### Lack of Current Federal Recidivism Statistics

As previously noted, the only national-level recidivism statistics concerning the reentry of prisoners into the community are more than a decade old. These studies showed that over two- thirds of ex-offenders had come into contact with the legal system—either through a new arrest, a violation of the terms of their release, or a new conviction—within three years of their release. However, there are no current national-level recidivism statistics. While a number of states have conducted studies of their prisoners' recidivism, the lack of national-level statistics poses a challenge for policy makers as they consider the issue of offender reentry. Without a current, national-level analysis of which ex-offenders are more likely to recidivate, it is difficult to target funding to offender reentry programs that address the at-risk population. Indeed, much of the offender reentry literature being published today continues to cite the Bureau of Justice Statistics study from the mid-1990s when referring to recidivism. A potential issue of interest for Congress may be whether a new, national-level recidivism study is needed to better understand the current trends in recidivism and to better target federal funding to the ex-offenders that are most likely to re-offend.

## OFFENDER REENTRY: A BRIEF LITERATURE REVIEW

Virtually all prisoners currently being detained in secure facilities will, someday, be released into the community, and more offenders are transitioning into the community today than ever before. Offender reentry is a complex issue that touches on a wide range of social and governmental networks and programs. Offender reentry policies can vary significantly from state to state, and from community to community within particular states. The policies affecting prisoners and the kinds of programs available to them both in and out of prison depend on a variety of factors, including the availability of funding for social programs within states and communities and the number of private non-profit and religious organizations operating in a given community. The federal government plays a supporting role through the numerous grant funding opportunities (discussed below). Complicating factors affecting how offender reentry works in a given community can include

- the varying types of sentences handed down,
- the different kinds of release mechanisms available to judges,
- the types of programs provided in prisons by correctional systems,
- the intensity of supervision provided or required by the parole or releasing agency,
- the family and community support available to the offender,
- the kinds of social services available in the offender's community, and
- the status of the local economy and the offender's ability to obtain employment.[30]

## Offender Reentry Defined

Before we can discuss offender reentry programs, however, it is useful to comment on what constitutes offender reentry. Some observers note that offender reentry is the natural byproduct of incarceration, because all prisoners who are not sentenced to life in prison and who do not die in prison will reenter the community at some point. According to this school of thought, reentry is not a program or some kind of legal status but rather a process that almost all offenders will undergo.[31] A variant on this approach to reentry is the concept that offender reentry, "simply defined, includes all activities and programming conducted to prepare ex-convicts to return safely to the community and to live as law abiding citizens."[32] The basic idea here is that every activity and process that a prisoner undergoes while in the judicial and correctional systems will have some nexus with their reentry into the community.

Although this broad definition of reentry certainly encompasses all the activities that may impinge on or affect a prisoner's reentry into society, it may be a cumbersome one for the purposes of crafting and evaluating government policies. For example, it is difficult, if not impossible, to measure the outcome of a reentry program if one includes in the definition of reentry every activity that a prisoner undergoes during his time in the criminal justice system. This has led many in the field to focus on a more narrow and thus more manageable definition of reentry. This more narrow definition is often stated in two parts: correctional programs that focus on the transition to the community (such as prerelease, work release, halfway houses, or other programs specifically aiming at reentry) and programs that have initiated some form of treatment (such as substance abuse, life skills, education, or mental health) in prison that is linked to community programs that will continue the treatment once the prisoner has been released.[33] Narrowing the definition of reentry thusly allows policy makers to focus on programs that expressly aim to manage the transition from detention to the community.

## Program Effectiveness: The "What Works" Literature

Compared with other social science fields, there has been a relative lack of rigorously designed studies on the issue of offender reentry. Nevertheless, in recent years, there has been increasing attention on this issue and a number of new studies have been published. This has allowed academics to undertake some of the first broad meta-analyses[34] of offender reentry studies. Some of these studies have hewn closely to the "what works" paradigm created by University of Maryland researchers for a National Institute of Justice report to Congress.[35] This concept was adapted to the field of offender reentry in a 2003 St. Louis University Study.[36] The "what works" literature attempts to identify programs that are effective by creating a scoring system to evaluate studies based on whether they can be proven to have an impact. Inherent to this approach is the need to identify program evaluations that provide evidence concerning the effect the program had on certain outcome measures. The "what works" paradigm essentially focuses on whether studies have accomplished the following things:

- controlled for variables in their analysis that may have been the underlying cause of any observed connection between the program being studied and the outcome measures being analyzed;
- determined whether there are measurement errors resulting from problems with the study, including such things as participants being lost over time or low response rates to interview requests; and
- calculated the statistical power of the analysis to detect the program's effects on outcome measures. Included in this category are things such as sample size and the base rate of crime in the community.[37]

The "what works" model uses these core criteria to place studies into five distinct categories, with category 5 being the most scientifically rigorous, and thus considered most effective, studies. The model then uses this criteria to identify programs that, based on the evidence considered, have been proven to work, programs that are promising, and programs that do not work.

Following is a brief discussion of the types of offender reentry programs that have been judged to be effective in the "what works" literature, as well as in other studies. It is important to note here that just because a program has been reported to work in one location, or for a certain population, does not necessarily mean that it can be just as effective in other locations or among other populations. A number of factors can impinge on a program's effectiveness in any given location. For example, while knowing that a program has worked in the past can provide a model or blueprint to guide policy practitioners in other locations, how a program is implemented is just as important to its ultimate success as the underlying model that it is based on. The most effective model program can be compromised if it is not implemented properly. In addition, geographic, demographic, and other differences between locations can affect whether a program that succeeded in one place succeeds in another. Nevertheless, knowing that a program has worked in the past is of use to policy makers as they consider where to allocate funding and other resources.

### *Employment*

There are a number of studies that demonstrate that employment is a fundamental component of the reentry process, and that ex-offenders who are able to find stable employment are much more likely to succeed in their rehabilitation than those who cannot find work.[38] Several vocational and work programs were found to effectively reduce recidivism and improve the job-readiness of ex- offenders by the "what works" review.[39]

### *Drug Treatment*

Drug rehabilitation and treatment have also been found to be effective by a number of different studies, including the "what works" literature. These studies showed that, for recidivism and drug-use relapse, drug treatment can significantly improve outcome measures. In general, programs that provide intensive treatment in prison, combined and integrated with aftercare programs, have been shown to be effective in reducing recidivism and substance abuse among their participants—especially for offenders with serious crime and substance abuse histories.[40]

### *Halfway House Programs*

A number of programs that provide transitional housing for ex-offenders as they begin their transition into the community have been found to be effective. Offenders participating in halfway house programs were found to commit fewer and less severe offenses than those who did not participate. Participants also performed better on a range of other outcome measures, such as finding and holding a job, being self-supporting, and participating in self-improvement programs; however, these results were not statistically significant.[41]

### *Other Kinds of Programs*

The "what works" review concluded that other programs were either not effective or had not been studied enough for firm conclusions to be drawn. Education programs, for example, were found to raise educational achievement scores but not to reduce recidivism. Pre-release programs and programs focusing on violent offenders and sex offenders showed some evidence that they were effective in reducing recidivism, but few of these kinds of studies made it through the selection process. This precluded any firm conclusions from being drawn about these kinds of programs and pointed to the need for more evaluations.[42]

### *Limitations of the "What Works" Literature*

One of the main limitations associated with the "what works" literature is the dearth of studies that meet its rigorous requirements. For example, the offender reentry study cited above was only able to identify 32 studies that met its selection criteria. Only 19 of these program evaluations contained a comparison, or control, group, and of these, only 2 were randomized control trials.[43] This has led some to question whether the programs identified to work by this literature review are, in fact, effective.[44] Moreover, most of the studies identified by the "what works" literature evaluate program effectiveness based almost entirely on recidivism. As previously noted, some believe other outcome measures may be just as important in deciding whether a program has been effective in reintegrating ex-offenders into their communities. Lastly, evaluations that incorporate random assignment and provide statistically rigorous results are, by and large, expensive. This means that policy makers are often confronted with hard decisions concerning whether to fund additional services or evaluations of existing programs.

## *Conclusion*

After reviewing the available literature, some patterns appear to emerge. Many of the programs that have been proven to be effective share some of the same attributes, regardless of whether they focus on vocational training, substance abuse prevention, mental health services, or alternative housing. The attributes shared by most of these programs include the following:

- they start during institutional placement, but take place mostly in the community;
- they are intensive in nature, lasting typically at least six months;
- they focus services on individuals determined to be at high risk of recidivating through the use of risk-assessment classifications; and
- if they are treatment programs, they use cognitive-behavioral treatment techniques, matching particular therapists and programs to the specific learning characteristics of the offenders.[45]

# FEDERAL OFFENDER REENTRY PROGRAMS

Following is a brief description of the main federal programs that have been used to help state and local entities to fund activities relating to the reintegration of ex-offenders into local communities. It is important to note that some of these programs may no longer be receiving funding; these programs are identified below. Other programs that are currently funded may not provide funding for offender reentry purposes every fiscal year. Nevertheless, these programs have been included to provide a comprehensive look at the universe of federal resources that could be used for offender reentry purposes.

## Offender Reentry Programs at the Department of Justice (DOJ)

The first reentry-specific program at the DOJ was the Serious and Violent Offender Reentry Initiative (SVORI), which was coordinated by the Office of Justice Programs (OJP). The SVORI was a federal offender reentry pilot program for adult offenders that focused on coordinating the way federal agencies distribute offender reentry funding. The main federal agencies involved were the Departments of Justice, Labor, Education, and Housing and

Urban Development. As part of SVORI, their objective was to help state and local agencies navigate the wide array of existing state formula and block grants and to assist the states and communities to leverage those resources to create comprehensive offender reentry programs. The program distributed $110 million to 69 grantees and concluded in FY2005.

An evaluation of SVORI programs was released in December 2009.[46] The evaluation, among other things, evaluated the post-release outcomes of participants in 16 programs (12 adult and 4 juvenile) in 14 states.[47] The evaluation found that there was little difference in the reported reentry programming needs between offenders who participated in SVORI programs and those who did not participate. Inmates who participated in SVORI programs were more likely to receive reentry programming and services than those who did not participate, but not all SVORI program participants received programming or services.

The researchers also found that the provision of services for program participants was below the expressed need for services. Moreover, the provision of services decreased after the inmates were released from confinement.

The researchers found that adults who participated in the SVORI program were moderately more likely than non-participants to find housing and employment, not use drugs, and self-report less criminal behavior. However, improvement on these measures (i.e., housing, employment, drug use, and criminal behavior) did not translate into lower levels of reincarceration. Juvenile males who participated in SVORI programs were more likely than non-participants to have a job with benefits 15 months after being released, but there was no significant difference between program participants and non-participants in terms of substance abuse, physical health, mental health, or recidivism.

The Prisoner Reentry Initiative (PRI) was the successor to the SVORI program. According to OJP, the PRI provided funding for model offender reentry programs that focused on providing services and assistance during the three phases of offender reentry: at detention facilities, just prior to and after the offender's release, and during an ex-offender's long-term transition to the community. Congress discontinued funding the PRI after FY2008.

From FY2001 to FY2003, Congress appropriated funding for the DOJ portion of the SVORI under the Community Oriented Policing Services account in the annual Commerce, Justice, Science, and Related Agencies appropriations act.

Appropriations were provided during these fiscal years even though they were not authorized. As a part of the 21$^{st}$ Century Department of Justice Reauthorization Act of 2002 (P.L. 107-273), Congress authorized appropriations for an adult and juvenile offender reentry demonstration program.

The act originally authorized appropriations of $15.0 million for FY2003, $15.5 million for FY2004, and $16.0 million for FY2005. For FY2004 to FY2008, Congress appropriated funding for the SVORI and the PRI pursuant to the authorization for the adult and juvenile offender reentry demonstration program.

The Second Chance Act of 2007 (P.L. 110-199)[48] reauthorized and modified the scope of the adult and juvenile offender reentry demonstration program. The act replaced the previous four purpose areas eligible for funding with new purpose areas spanning every phase of the offender reentry process. Applicants for these grants are subject to a number of requirements, including submitting a reentry strategic plan with their application, describing the long-term strategy, and providing a detailed implementation schedule, among other things.

The act requires that states and localities match 50% of the federal funds provided; up to half of this state match (or 25% of the overall total funding) can be composed of in-kind contributions. The act also created some new demonstration grant programs, including

- grants for state and local reentry courts;
- grants for drug treatment diversion programs;
- grants to expand substance-abuse programs for prisoners and ex-offenders; and
- grants to expand the use of career training programs and mentoring programs.

Since FY2009, funding DOJ for reentry programs has been appropriated pursuant to the grant programs authorized by the Second Chance Act.

## Offender Reentry Programs at Other Federal Agencies

As previously mentioned, many federal departments provide funding through a wide array of programs and block grants, which can be used by states for offender reentry. The following list is not meant to be an exhaustive one, but it does capture many programs run by other departments that can be used to support state offender reentry initiatives.

### *The Department of Labor (DOL)*

The Workforce Investment Act[49] (WIA) of 1998 (P.L. 105-220) authorized a nationwide system of workforce development programs, America's Workforce Network, that provides information and services to connect youths and adults with employers.[50] These programs, which can be used by ex-offenders, provide services such as skills-training and job-placement. DOL also instituted a Young Offender Reentry Demonstration Grant Program, which provides funds to communities for offender reentry programs for offenders aged 14 to 21 who are already in the criminal justice system or are considered high-risk. This program focuses on job-training, education, substance- abuse treatment, mental health care, housing assistance, and family support services.

In addition, DOL maintains two programs that provide incentives for companies to hire ex- offenders. The Work Opportunity Tax Credits program[51] provides up to $2,400 in tax credits to companies for every former offender they hire,[52] and the Federal Bonding Program[53] allows companies who cannot obtain bonding or insurance from their own providers to bond ex- offenders for up to $25,000 for up to six months.[54]

**Table 1. Authorized and Appropriated Funding for the DOJ Reentry Program, FY2001-FY2008 (in thousands of dollars)**

|  | Authorized | Appropriated |
|---|---|---|
| FY2001 | N.A. | $29,934 |
| FY2002 | N.A. | 14,934 |
| FY2003 | 15,000 | 14,837 |
| FY2004 | 15,500 | 4,947 |
| FY2005 | 16,000 | 9,866 |
| FY2006 | N.A. | 4,936 |
| FY2007 | N.A. | 14,879 |
| FY2008 | N.A. | 11,750 |

Source: Data provided by the U.S. Department of Justice, Community Oriented Policing Services Office.

Notes: "N.A." means "not authorized."

**Table 2. Authorized and Appropriated Funding for the Second Chance Act Grant Programs Administered by the Department of Justice, FY2009-FY2013**

**Appropriations and authorizations in thousands of dollars**

| | FY2009 | | FY2010 | | FY2011 | | FY2012 | | FY2013 | |
|---|---|---|---|---|---|---|---|---|---|---|
| | Authorized | Appropriated | Authorized | Appropriated | Authorized | Appropriated | Authorized | Appropriated | Authorized | Appropriated |
| Adult and Juvenile Offender Reentry Demonstration Program | $55,000 | $15,000 | $55,000 | $37,000 | N.A. | $30,649 | N.A. | Unknown | N.A. | Unknown |
| State and Local Reentry Courts | 10,000 | — | 10,000 | 10,000 | N.A. | 8,283 | N.A. | Unknown | N.A. | Unknown |
| Drug Treatment Alternative to Prison Programs | 10,000 | — | 10,000 | — | N.A. | — | N.A. | Unknown | N.A. | Unknown |
| Family Substance Abuse Treatment Alternative to Incarceration Grants | 10,000 | — | 10,000 | 7,500 | N.A. | 6,213 | N.A. | Unknown | N.A. | Unknown |
| Grants to Evaluate and Improve Education Methods at Prison, Jails, and Juvenile Facilities | 5,000 | — | 5,000 | 2,500 | N.A. | 2,071 | N.A. | Unknown | N.A. | Unknown |
| Technology Careers Training Demonstration Grants | 10,000 | — | 10,000 | 5,000 | N.A. | 4,142 | N.A. | Unknown | N.A. | Unknown |
| Offender Reentry Substance Abuse and Criminal Justice Collaboration Program | 15,000 | — | 15,000 | 13,000 | N.A. | 10,768 | N.A. | Unknown | N.A. | Unknown |

| | FY2009 | | FY2010 | | FY2011 | | FY2012 | | FY2013 | |
|---|---|---|---|---|---|---|---|---|---|---|
| | Authorized | Appropriated | Authorized | Appropriated | Authorized | Appropriated | Authorized | Appropriated | Authorized | Appropriated |
| Mentoring Grants to Nonprofit Organizations | 15,000 | 10,000 | 15,000 | 15,000 | N.A. | 12,425 | N.A. | Unknown | N.A. | Unknown |
| Grants for Offender Reentry Research | 10,000 | — | 10,000 | 10,000 | N.A. | 8,283 | N.A. | Unknown | N.A. | Unknown |
| Smart Probation | N.A. | — | N.A. | — | N.A. | — | N.A. | 4,000 | N.A. | 4,649 |
| **Total** | **160,000** | **25,000** | **160,000** | **115,000** | **N.A.** | **97,774** | **N.A.** | **63,000**[a] | **N.A.** | **63,930**[b] |

Source: FY2009 appropriations were taken from P.L. 111-8; FY2010 appropriations were taken from P.L. 111-117; FY2011 appropriations were based on a CRS analysis of the text of P.L. 112-10; FY2012 appropriations were taken from P.L. 112-55; and FY2013 appropriations were provided by the Department of Justice.

Notes: "N.A." means "not authorized."

[a] For FY2012, $63 million was provided for DOJ-administered grant programs authorized under the Second Chance Act. Under the Consolidated and Further Continuing Appropriations Act, 2012 (P.L. 112-55), of which $4 million was set aside for a smart probation program. Congress allowed the Administration to decide how the remaining $59 million would be allocated between the programs authorized under the act.

[b] For FY2013, $63.9 million was provided for DOJ-administered grant programs authorized under the Second Chance Act. Under the Consolidated and Further Continuing Appropriations Act, 2013 (P.L. 113-6), of which $4.6 million was set aside for a smart probation program. Congress allowed the Administration to decide how the remaining $63.8 million would be allocated between the programs authorized under the act. The FY2013 enacted amount includes a 1.877% rescission per section 3001 of P.L. 113-6 and a 0.2% rescission ordered by the Office of Management and Budget per section 3004 of P.L. 113-6. The FY2013 enacted amount also includes the amount sequestered per the Budget Control Act of 2011(P.L. 112-25).

## The Department of Education (DOE)

A variety of DOE programs can be used by states to help fund or provide technical support for offender reentry programs that focus on education. The Office of Vocational and Adult Education provides several different programs for offender reentry. The Lifeskills for State and Local Inmates Program provides funding for demonstration projects to reduce recidivism through educational services before inmates are discharged into the community.[55] The Grants to States for Workplace and Community Transition Training for Incarcerated Youth Offenders funds postsecondary education and vocational training to people under the age of 25 from five years before their release to one year post-release.[56] Title II of the Workforce Investment Act, Adult Education and Family Literacy, also authorized funding to be appropriated for basic skills instruction; up to 10% of the funds can be used for institutionalized offenders or for ex-offenders in community programs. In addition, the Perkins State Grant Program allows states to use up to 1% of their funds to serve offenders in institutions.[57]

## The Department of Housing and Urban Development (HUD)

HUD funds a variety of programs that help states and local governments to support housing programs. The Community Development Block Grant Program aims to assist states in developing viable urban communities. Funds are allocated by formula to the states, and communities and grantees have significant discretion concerning how to allocate their federal funding— including using some funds to provide housing for ex-offenders.[58]

## The Department of Health and Human Services (DHHS)

DHHS provides funding for a multitude of programs that can be used to help offender reentry programs through the Substance Abuse and Mental Health Services Agency[59] (SAMHSA) and the Office of Community Services. These programs include the Recovery Community Support Program, which targets people and families recovering from drug abuse and addiction, and several block grant programs. SAMHSA also funds a program that specifically targets offender reentry known as the Young Offender Reentry Program (YORP). The YORP provides funding for state, tribal, and local governments, as well as community based non-profit organizations, to expand substance abuse treatment and supervision programs for juvenile and young adult offenders re-entering the community.[60] Funds for DHHS programs may be used to provide substance abuse or mental health services for offenders on parole or probation. However, DHHS funds may not used to provide services to incarcerated offenders.[61]

## Coordination between Federal Agencies

There are a number of entities that bring together offender reentry professionals from state and local governments, non-profit organizations, and academic institutions, including the Reentry Policy Council founded by the Council of State Governments and the Reentry Roundtable hosted by the Urban Institute. Both of these organizations attempt to bolster information sharing about best practices and funding opportunities and coordination between the various state and local agencies and stake-holders within the offender reentry field.

The DOJ has started an interagency Reentry Council to coordinate federal reentry efforts and advance effective reentry policies. The first meeting of the council was held in January 2011, and one will be held every six months. The purpose of the council is "to bring together numerous federal agencies to make communities safer, assist those returning from prison and jail in becoming productive, tax-paying citizens, and save taxpayer dollars by lowering the direct and collateral costs of incarceration."[62] The council includes representatives from the following agencies and offices:

- Department of Justice,
- Department of the Interior,
- Department of Agriculture,
- Department of Labor,
- Department of Health and Human Services,
- Department of Housing and Urban Development,
- Department of Education,
- Department of Veterans Affairs,
- Office of National Drug Control Policy,
- Social Security Administration,
- Domestic Policy Council,
- Equal Employment Opportunity Commission,
- White House Office of Faith-Based and Neighborhood Partnerships,
- Office of Personnel Management,
- Office of Management and Budget,

- Internal Revenue Service,
- Federal Trade Commission,
- Interagency Council on Homelessness, and
- Small Business Administration.

## CONCLUSION

Over the past two and a half decades, the prison population and the number of ex-offenders being released into the community have been increasing. The increasing number of ex-offenders entering the community has put pressure on public policy makers to provide treatments and services that will smooth the reintegration process while reducing recidivism. When deciding what programs to fund, policy makers often focus on reducing recidivism. The focus on reducing recidivism, however, is complicated by the fact that there are different definitions of recidivism. For example, the last major national-level study showed that two-thirds of ex-offenders came into contact with the legal system and that about half were back in prison within three years of their release. However, only a quarter of the ex-offenders ended up in prison for having committed new crimes; another quarter were back in prison for technical violations of their release (such as failing a drug test). Whether technical violations should be considered a measure of recidivism or whether recidivism should be confined to the commission of new crimes has engendered much debate within the criminal justice field.

While the emphasis on reducing recidivism is important, programs can also be evaluated based on other outcome measures such as their ability to connect ex-offenders with jobs, services, and institutions in their communities. The best available research has shown that there are a number of services that can help ex-offenders reconnect with their communities and lower recidivism, including programs focusing on providing vocational training, substance abuse prevention, mental health services, and alternative housing. The reportedly most successful programs focus on high-risk offenders, are intensive in nature, begin during institutional placement, and take place mostly in the community. However, a relative lack of scientifically rigorous research has made it difficult to draw definitive conclusions about which programs are most effective.

As Congress considers this issue, a number of policy issues may be assessed, including whether the current federal grant programs are adequate or whether new programs should be created, whether there is a need for more current national-level recidivism data, whether enough coordination of the many programs that may be used to help ex-offenders is occurring within the federal government, whether more evaluations of offender reentry programs are needed, and whether funding will be appropriated for the programs and activities that were authorized by the Second Chance Act.

# APPENDIX. SECTION-BY-SECTION COMPARISON OF THE SECOND CHANCE ACT

The Second Chance Act, P.L. 110-199, was passed by the House on November 13, 2007, and by the Senate on March 11, 2008. The act was signed into law on April 9, 2008. Following is a section-by-section analysis of the act's provisions.

## Amendments to Current Offender Reentry Grant Program (§101)

The Second Chance Act reauthorized and expanded the adult and juvenile offender state and local offender reentry demonstration projects codified at 42 U.S.C. 3797w(b-c). The act replaced the four current purpose areas eligible for funding with seven broad purpose areas:

- educational, literacy, vocational, and job placement services;
- substance abuse treatment and services, including programs that start in placement and continue through the community;
- programs that provide comprehensive supervision and offer services in the community, including programs that provide housing assistance and mental and physical health services;
- programs that focus on family integration during and after placement for both offenders and their families;
- mentoring programs that start in placement and continue into the community;
- programs that provide victim-appropriate services, including those that promote the timely payment of restitution by offenders and those that offer services (such as security or counseling) to victims when offenders are released; and

- programs that protect communities from dangerous offenders, including developing and implementing the use of risk assessment tools to determine when offenders should be released from prison.

Applicants for these grants are subjected to a number of requirements, including submitting a reentry strategic plan with their application, describing the long-term strategy, providing a detailed implementation schedule, identifying the local government's role in the plan, and describing the "evidence based methodology and outcome measures" that are used to evaluate the programs and "provide valid measures" of the program's impact.

The act allows the Attorney General (AG) to make grants for these programs if the applications received meet the following conditions:

- they are explicitly supported by the chief executive of the unit of government applying for the funding;
- they extensively discuss the role that the various law enforcement entities involved in the reentry process will have in the program;
- they provide extensive evidence of collaboration among the state and local health, housing, child welfare, education, substance abuse, victims services, employment, and law enforcement agencies;
- they provide a plan for analyzing any statutory, regulatory, or other hurdles that may exist to reintegrating offenders into the community; and
- they include a reentry taskforce as described below to carry out the activities funded under the grant.

The act requires applicants to develop a comprehensive strategic reentry plan that contains measurable five-year performance outcomes, with the goal of reducing recidivism by 50% over this period. As a condition of funding, applicants are also required to create offender reentry taskforces that would integrate the prime offender reentry stake-holders in their communities in order to pool resources, facilitate data-collection, and reduce recidivism. Grantees are also required to submit annual reports to DOJ that identify the specific progress made toward achieving their strategic performance outcomes, and may be eligible for future grants if they demonstrate adequate progress towards reducing recidivism by 10% over a two-year period.

In awarding grants under this program, the AG is directed to prioritize applications that

- focus on geographic areas with a disproportionate population of ex-offenders;
- include input from non-profit organizations, consultation with victims and ex- offenders, and coordinate with families;
- demonstrate effective case management in order to provide comprehensive and continuous services during reentry;
- review the adjudications process for parole violations in the applicant's criminal justice system;
- provide for an independent evaluation of the program, including, to the extent practicable, the use of random assignment; and
- target high risk offenders through the use of validated assessment tools.

Additionally, the act establishes a National Adult and Juvenile Offender Reentry Resource Center by authorizing the AG to make a grant available to an eligible organization. The selected organization are directed to provide education, training, and technical assistance to states and other governments in order to collect and disseminate data and best practices in offender reentry, including the use of evaluation tools and other measures to assess and document performance. Up to 4% of the authorized level of funding can be used to establish and run this center.

The act authorizes $55 million in both FY2009 and FY2010 for these programs and limits funding for technical assistance and training to between 2% and 3% of the overall total appropriated. The total federal share of funding for these grants is limited to 50%; however, up to 50% of the state and local matching funds (i.e., 25% of the overall grant) could be fulfilled through in-kind contributions of goods or services.

## Improvement of the Residential Substance Abuse Treatment for State Offenders Program (§102)

This provision requires states receiving grants under the residential substance abuse treatment program (42 U.S.C. 3796ff) to ensure that individuals participating in these programs receive aftercare services, including a full continuum of support services. The act defines residential substance abuse treatment programs as a course of comprehensive individual and group substance abuse services lasting at least six months in residential treatment facilities that are set apart from the general population of a prison or jail. The act also requires the AG to study the use and effectiveness of the funds used to provide the required aftercare services.

## Definition of Violent Offender for Drug Court Program (§103)

The act modifies the government's current drug court grant program, restricting the current definition of "violent offender" to individuals charged with or convicted for certain offenses that are punishable by a sentence of longer than one year (prior there was no minimum sentence length).[63] The act requires all grantees under this program to adhere to this definition of "violent offender" within three years of the enactment of the act (i.e., April 9, 2011), and requires the secretary to publish regulations to this effect within 90 days of enactment. Any drug court not adhering to this definition by April 9, 2011, would see their grant allocations reduced.

## New Offender Reentry Grant Programs

Subtitle B creates a number of new targeted grant programs within the Department of Justice (DOJ) relating to the reintegration of offenders into the community.

## State and Local Reentry Courts (§111)

This provision creates a new grant program within DOJ to fund reentry courts. Subject to the availability of appropriations, grants up to $500,000 are made available for state and local adult and juvenile court systems in order to establish and maintain reentry courts. These courts will be tasked with monitoring juvenile and adult offenders reentering into the community and providing them with a coordinated and comprehensive array of services, including housing assistance, education, job training, health services, and substance abuse treatment. In order to be eligible for funding, applicants have to demonstrate the need for their program; create a long-term strategy and detailed implementation plan; identify the government and community entities that would be coordinated by the project; and describe the methodology and outcome measures that would be used to evaluate the program. Additionally, applicants are required to submit annual reports to DOJ including a summary of the activities carried out with the grant and an assessment of whether these activities are meeting the needs identified in the grant application. The act authorizes $10 million for this program in FY2009 and FY2010. The total federal share of funding for these grants is limited to 50%; however, up to 50% of the state and local matching funds (i.e., 25% of the overall grant) could be fulfilled through in-kind contributions of goods or services.

## Drug Treatment Alternative to Prison Programs (§112)

This provision creates a new grant program for state and local prosecutors to fund the development, implementation, and expansion of drug treatment programs that are alternatives to imprisonment. The programs require eligible offenders, after having received the consent of the prosecutor, to participate in comprehensive drug treatment programs in lieu of imprisonment. Criminal charges would be dismissed upon completion of the program. Offenders failing to successfully complete their treatment programs would serve their original sentence. In order to be eligible for these programs, the offender in question could not have had any prior felony use of force convictions or have been charged with or convicted of an offense involving a firearm, a dangerous weapon, or the use of force against another individual. The act authorizes $10 million for this program in FY2009 and FY2010. The total federal share of funding for these grants is limited to 50%; however, up to 50% of the state and local matching funds (i.e., 25% of the overall grant) could be fulfilled through in-kind contributions of goods or services.

## Family Substance Abuse Treatment Alternatives to Incarceration Grants (§113)

This provision creates a new grant program to develop, implement, and expand the use of family- based substance abuse treatment programs as alternatives to incarceration for non-violent parent drug offenders. Among other things, the treatment is required to be clinically appropriate, comprehensive, and long-term and would be provided in a residential setting rather than an outpatient or a hospital setting. The program is required to include the implementation of graduated sanctions applied on the basis of the offender's accountability throughout the course of the program and the development of reentry plans for offenders. Offenders failing to complete the program are required to complete the sentence for the underlying crime involved. Grantees are required to submit annual reports to DOJ detailing the effectiveness of their programs using evidence-based data. Prison-based programs are required to locate their programs in an area separate from the general population, to create and support treatment plans for incarcerated parents, and to ensure continuity of care if participating offenders are transferred to a different facility. The act authorizes $10 million in FY2009 and in FY2010 for these grants; not less than 5% of this total is to be allocated to Indian Tribes.

## Grants to Evaluate and Improve Educational Methods at Prisons, Jails, and Juvenile Facilities (§114)

This program authorizes the AG, subject to the availability of appropriations, to make grants to evaluate, identify, and improve programs that focus on providing educational and vocational programs for offenders by identifying and implementing best practices. Grantees are required to submit reports within 90 days of the last day of the final fiscal year of a grant detailing the progress that they have made. The act authorizes appropriations of $5 million for this program in FY2009 and FY2010.

## Technology Careers Training Demonstration Grants

The act authorizes the AG to make grants to states, units of local governments, territories, and Indian Tribes to provide technology career training for prisoners. Grants may be awarded for programs that establish technology careers training programs for offenders during the three-year period prior to their release. Access to the Internet during the program will be restricted to ensure public safety. Grantees must submit a report to DOJ describing and assessing the program each fiscal year. The act authorizes $10 million for this program in FY2009 and FY2010.

## New Drug-Treatment and Mentoring Grant Programs

Title II of P.L. 110-199 authorizes a series of new grant programs for drug-treatment and mentoring purposes. Subtitle A (§201) focuses on drug treatment programs, Subtitles B and C (§§211-214) focus on training and mentoring programs, and Subtitle C (§231) would create a federal offender reentry program at the Bureau of Prisons.

## Offender Reentry Substance Abuse and Criminal Justice Collaboration Program (§201)

The act authorizes the AG to make grants to states, units of local governments, territories, and Indian Tribes in order to improve drug treatment programs in prisons and reduce the use of alcohol and other drugs by long-term abusers under correctional supervision. Grants may be used to continue or improve existing drug treatment programs, develop and implement programs for long-term substance abusers, provide addiction recovery support services, and establish pharmacological drug treatment services as part of any drug treatment program offered to prisoners.[64] Grant applicants are required to identify the entities that will be involved in providing the treatment, certify that this treatment has been developed in consultation with the Single State Authority for Substance Abuse,[65] certify that the treatment will be clinically appropriate and will provide comprehensive treatment, and describe how evidence-based strategies have been incorporated into the program, including the collection and analysis of data. The AG is required to submit a report to Congress detailing best practices relating to substance abuse treatment in prison and comprehensive treatment of long-term substance abusers by September 30, 2009. Another report on the drug treatment programs funded through this grant program is required by September 30, 2010. The act authorizes appropriations of $15 million for this program in both FY2009 and FY2010.

## Mentoring Grants to Nonprofit Organizations (§211)

This provision would create a new grant program to provide mentoring and other transitional services for offenders being released into the community. Funding could be used for mentoring programs both in placement and during reentry, programs providing transition services during reentry, and programs providing training for "offender and victims issues." Priority would be given to applicants providing for the evaluation of their programs, using randomized control trials to the maximum extent feasible. Applicants would be required to identify and report on specific outcome performance measures related to the overall goal of reducing recidivism. The bills would authorize $15 million in FY2009 and in FY2010 for these grants.

## Responsible Reintegration of Offenders (§212)

The act authorizes the Secretary of Labor to make grants to non-profit organizations to provide a wide array of mentoring, job training and job placement services, and other comprehensive transitional services. Grants may not be used to provide substance abuse treatment, mental health treatment, or housing services; however, grants can be used to coordinate with other entities providing these services. Applications for the program must identify the specific eligible area that will be served and the need for support in this area and describe the services that will be provided, the partnerships that have been established with the criminal justice system and housing authorities, and how other sources of funding will be leveraged to provide support services. In order to be eligible for funding, programs must be located in urbanized areas or clusters (as determined by the Bureau of the Census) that have a large number of prisoners returning to the community and high recidivism rates (however, no definitions for a large number of returning prisoners or high recidivism rates are provided). To be eligible for the program, offenders would be at least 18 years old, have no prior adult convictions or convictions for violent or sex-related offenses, and have been released from prison no more than 180 days before they begin participating in the grant program.[66] Not more than 15% of the grant may be used to pay for administrative costs. The act authorizes $20 million in appropriations for the Secretary of Labor to carry out this section in both FY2009 and FY2010; up to 4% of the appropriation may be used to provide technical assistance.

## Bureau of Prisons Policies on Mentoring Contacts (§213)

This provision directs the Director of the Bureau of Prisons (BOP) at DOJ to adopt and implement a policy by July 9, 2009, to ensure that mentors working with incarcerated offenders are permitted to continue providing their services to the offender after their release from prison. The Director is required to submit a report to Congress concerning this policy's implementation by September 20, 2009.

## Bureau of Prisons Policies on Chapel Library Material (§214)

The Director of the BOP is required to discontinue the Standardized Chapel Library project, or any other project that compiles, lists, or restricts prisoner access to materials provided by chapel libraries by May 9, 2008. Exceptions are made for materials that incite, promote, or suggest violence and materials prohibited by law.

## Federal Prisoner Reentry Program (§231)

The act establishes a prisoner reentry program within the BOP. BOP is required to create a federal prisoner reentry strategy that will

- assess each prisoner's skill level at the beginning of their prison term (including academic, vocational, health, cognitive, interpersonal, daily living, and other related skills);
- create a skills development plan for prisoners to be carried out during their term of imprisonment;
- determine program assignments for prisoners based on the needs identified by the assessment;
- give priority to the reentry needs of high-risk populations, including sex- offenders, career criminals, and prisoners with mental health problems;
- coordinate and collaborate with other criminal justice, community-based, and faith-based organizations;
- collect information about a prisoner's family relationships and parental responsibilities; and
- provide incentives for prisoners to participate in skills development programs.

Incentives for prisoners to participate in skills development programs include allowing offenders to spend the maximum amount of time in community confinement facilities. Additionally, BOP is required to assist offenders in obtaining identification prior to their release.

The act modifies current law to include a number of new duties for the Director of BOP. These new duties include the establishment of prerelease planning procedures for all federal offenders that help prisoners apply for federal and state benefits prior to their release, and the establishment of reentry planning procedures to provide federal offenders with information in a number of reentry-related areas. BOP is required to establish and implement a system that will allow it to quantitatively track progress in responding to the reentry needs of its inmates and to provide an annual report to the House and Senate Committees on the Judiciary concerning its progress. An annual report is also required containing recidivism statistics for federal prisoners, including information concerning the relative recidivism rates of offenders participating in major inmate programs. After the initial report establishes a baseline recidivism rate for BOP ex-offenders, the act establishes 5- and 10-year goals of 2% and 5% reductions in this rate, respectively.

BOP is further required to ensure that the United States Probation and Pretrial Services System has medical information for inmates scheduled for release in order to create supervision plans that address the medical and mental health care needs of ex-offenders, and to ensure that each prisoner in community confinement has access to medical and mental health care.

In addition to the offender reentry program established above, the act also establishes two new programs within BOP:

- A pilot program within BOP to determine the effectiveness of allowing certain elderly, non-violent offenders to serve the remainder of their sentences on home detention. In order to be eligible for this program, offenders would have to be 65 years old or older and have never been convicted of a violent or sex-related crime or given a life-sentence, among other things.
- A program to provide satellite tracking of certain high-risk individuals after their release from prison, in conjunction with the use of graduated sanctions, the provision of reentry related services, and the involvement the offender's family, a victim advocate, and the victim. The act authorizes $5 million for this purpose in FY2009 and in FY2010.

## Offender Reentry Research (§241)

The act allows, but does not direct, the National Institute of Justice to conduct research into offender reentry. This research may include a study identifying the number and characteristics of children with incarcerated parents and their likelihood of engaging in criminal activity, a study identifying mechanisms to compare recidivism rates between states, and a study on the characteristics of individuals released from prison who do not recidivate.

The act also allows, but does not direct, the Bureau of Justice Statistics to conduct research on offender reentry. This research may include an analysis of the populations that present unique reentry challenges, studies to determine the characteristics of individuals who return to prison (including which individuals pose the highest risk to the community), annual reports on the profile of the population leaving detention and entering the community, a national recidivism study every three years, and a study of post incarceration supervision (e.g., parole) violations.

## Grants to Study Post-Incarceration Supervision Violations (§242)

This provision creates a new grant program to fund state studies aimed at improving data- collection on offenders who have their post-incarceration supervision revoked in order to better identify which individuals pose the greatest risk to the community. In order to receive funding, states have to certify that their program would collect "comprehensive and reliable data" and have to provide this data to the Bureau of Justice Statistics.

## Addressing the Needs of Children of Incarcerated Parents (§243)

This provision directs the AG to collect data and develop best practices concerning the communication and coordination between state corrections and child welfare agencies, especially as they relate to the safety and support of children of incarcerated parents. The best practices developed should include policies, procedures, and programs that could be used to safeguard the parent-child bond during incarceration and assist incarcerated parents in planning for the future and well being of their children.

## Study of Effectiveness of Depot Naltrexone for Heroin Addiction (§244)

The act authorizes the AG, acting through the National Institute of Justice, to make grants to public and private research entities to evaluate the effectiveness of depot naltrexone for the treatment of heroin addiction. In order to be eligible for funding, research entities must demonstrate that they conduct research in a public or private institution of higher education, that they plan to work with parole or probation officers for offenders under court supervision, and that they will use randomized control trials to evaluate their programs. Grantees are required to submit reports to DOJ describing and assessing the uses of their grant.

## Authorization of Appropriations for Research (§245)

The act authorizes $10 million in both FY2009 and FY2010 to carry out the research programs authorized by §§241-244.

## Clarification of Authority to Place Prisoner in Community Corrections (§251)

This provision would require the Director of the BOP to ensure, to the extent practicable, that prisoners within the federal correctional system spend up to a year at the end of their sentence focusing on their reentry into the community. As part of this practice, BOP would be authorized to transfer offenders to community correctional facilities or to home confinement (for the shorter of the last 10% or six months of their sentence). The provision would also give BOP the discretion to disregard a court's order that an offender serve part of his sentence in a community correctional facility.

## Residential Drug Abuse Program in Federal Prisons (§252)

The act replaces the current definition of a residential drug abuse program with language defining such a program as a course of individual and group activities and treatment lasting at least six months in residential treatment facilities that are set apart from the general prison population. The act also stipulate that this treatment can include pharmacotherapies that extend beyond the six- month period.

## Contracting for Services for Post-Conviction Supervision of Offenders (§253)

This provision would give the Director of the Administrative Office of the United States Courts the authority to enter into contracts with public and private agencies to monitor and provide a wide array of services to offenders in the community to promote their reintegration.

## Extension of National Prison Rape Elimination Commission (§261)

The act extends the authorization for the National Prison Rape Elimination Commission[67] from three years to five years.

## End Notes

[1] U.S. Department of Justice, Office of Justice Programs, "Reentry," http://www.reentry.gov/.

[2] Paul Guerino, Paige M. Harrison, and William J. Sabol, *Prisoners in 2010*, U.S. Department of Justice, Office of Justice Programs, Bureau of Justice Statistics, NCJ 236096, Washington, DC, December 2011, p. 5, http://www.bjs.gov/content/pub/pdf/p10.pdf

[3] U.S. Department of Justice, Office of Justice Programs, Bureau of Justice Statistics, "Reentry Trends in the United States: Recidivism," available at http://www.ojp.usdoj.gov/bjs/reentry/recidivism.htm. Hereafter cited as "Reentry Trends."

[4] Wilkinson, Reginald A., Director of the Ohio Department of Rehabilitation and Correction, "Offender Reentry: A Storm Overdue," Paper Prepared for Third National Forum on Restorative Justice, March 2002, available at http://www.drc.state.oh.us/web/Articles/article98.htm. Hereafter cited as "A Storm Overdue."

[5] Tracey Kyckelhahn, *State Corrections Expenditures, FY1982-2010*, U.S. Department of Justice, Office of Justice Programs, Bureau of Justice Statistics, NCJ239672, Washington, DC, December 2012, p. 4, http://www.bjs.gov/ content/pub/pdf/scefy8210.pdf.

[6] Ibid., p. 11.

[7] U.S. Department of Justice, Office of Justice Programs, "Learn About Reentry," http://www.reentry.gov/learn.html. Hereafter cited as "Learn About Reentry."

[8] U.S. Government Accountability Office, "Prisoner Release: Trends and Information on Reintegration Programs," GAO-01-483, June 2001, pp. 19-25. Hereafter referred to as "GAO Prisoner Release Report."

[9] A Storm Overdue.

[10] Taxman, Faye et al., "Targeting for Reentry: Matching Needs and Services to Maximize Public Safety," National Criminal Justice Reference Service, March 25, 2002.

[11] GAO Prisoner Release Report, p. 5.

[12] While this is generally the case, jails on occasion can also include individuals sentenced to prison terms lasting less than one year (misdemeanors) and convicted felons in jurisdictions where the prisons are overpopulated.

[13] Reentry Trends.

[14] A determinate sentence is a fixed sentence, while an indeterminate sentence is typically expressed as a range (i.e., 5 to 10 years). For additional information on sentencing guidelines, please refer to CRS Report RL32766, *Federal Sentencing Guidelines: Background, Legal Analysis, and Policy Options*, by Lisa Seghetti and Alison M. Smith.

[15] U.S. Department of Justice, Bureau of Justice Statistics, *Truth in Sentencing in State Prisons*, NCJ170032, January 1999.

[16] For an expanded discussion of the varying definitions of recidivism, refer to Allen Beck, *Recidivism: A Fruit Salad Concept in the Criminal Justice World*, Justice Concepts, available at http://www.justiceconcepts.com/recidivism.pdf.

[17] See Colorado Department of Corrections, *Recidivism and Cumulative Return Rates: Calendar Year Releases from 1999 through 2005*, available at http://www.doc.state.co.us/Statistics/pdfs/Recidivism/2007RecidBulletin.pdf.

[18] See Florida Department of Corrections, *Recidivism Report: Inmates Released from Florida Prisons*, May 2001, available at http://www.dc.state.fl.us/pub/recidivism/2001/full.pdf.

[19] Patrick A. Langan and David J. Levin, United States Department of Justice, Bureau of Justice Statistics, *Recidivism of Prisoners Released in 1994*, Report NCJ193427, June 2002. Hereafter referred to as "1994 Recidivism Study."

[20] The states included in the study were Arizona, California, Delaware, Florida, Illinois, Maryland, Michigan, Minnesota, New Jersey, New York, North Carolina, Ohio, Oregon, Texas, and Virginia.

[21] 1994 Recidivism Study, p. 7.

[22] Pew Center on the States, *State of Recidivism: The Revolving Door of America's Prisons*, Washington, DC, April 2011, http://www.pewtrusts.org/uploadedFiles/wwwpewtrustsorg/Reports/sentencing_and_corrections/State_Recidivism_Revolving_Door_America_Prisons%20.pdf.

[23] Recidivism was defined as a return to prison, either for being convicted for a new crime or violating the terms of post-incarceration supervision. Ibid., p. 7.

[24] Pew notes that the high number of releases and rate of return for offenders from California has a significant effect on national recidivism rates, hence California was excluded from the comparison of recidivism rate for states that were included in both the BJS and Pew studies. Ibid., p. 12.

[25] United States Sentencing Commission, *A Comparison of the Federal Sentencing Guidelines Criminal History Category and the U.S. Parole Commission Salient Factor Score*.

[26] For examples of how the CHC system works within the federal sentencing guidelines, please refer to CRS Report RL32846, *How the Federal Sentencing Guidelines Work: Two Examples*, by Charles Doyle.

[27] Joan Petersilia, "What Works in Prisoner Reentry? Reviewing and Questioning the Evidence," *Federal Probation*, vol. 68, no. 2, 2004, pp. 4-8. Hereafter referred to as "Questioning the Evidence."

[28] Drug court programs typically divert nonviolent offenders arrested for drug-related crimes to treatment centers as opposed to prison.

[29] Questioning the Evidence, p. 7.

[30] Richard P. Seiter and Karen R. Kadela, "Prisoner Reentry: What Works, What Does Not, and What Is Promising," *Crime & Delinquency*, vol. 49, no. 3, 2003, pp. 360-388. Hereafter referred to as "Prisoner Reentry: What Works."

[31] Questioning the Evidence, 4-5.

[32] Questioning the Evidence, p. 5.

[33] Prisoner Reentry: What Works, p. 370.

[34] Meta-analyses are a type of systematic review of studies that allow researchers to draw conclusions across a wide range of studies by using statistical methods to derive quantitative results from the analysis of multiple sources of quantitative evidence.

[35] Lawrence W. Sherman, Denise Gottfredson, Doris MacKenzie, John Eck, Peter Reuter, and Shawn Bushway, *Preventing Crime: What Works, What Doesn't, What's Promising*, National Institute of Justice, 1997.

[36] Offender Reentry: What Works.

[37] Offender Reentry: What Works, pp. 370-373.

[38] See, for example, Shawn Bushway and Peter Reuter, "Labor Markets and Crime Risk Factors," in *Preventing Crime: What Works, What Doesn't, What's Promising. A Report to the United States Congress*, the National Institute of Justice, 1997, Chapter 6. Jeremy Travis, *But They All Come Back: Facing the Challenges of Prisoner Reentry*, The Urban Institute Press, 2005.

[39] Prisoner Reentry: What Works, pp. 373-374.

[40] Prisoner Reentry: What Works, p. 374.

[41] Prisoner Reentry: What Works, p. 378. A study's statistical significance is typically interpreted as a level of confidence (usually expressed as a probability, e.g., 95%) that an estimated impact is not merely the result of random variation, indicating that at least some of the measured impact may, with substantial confidence (e.g., 95% confidence), be attributed to the treatment as a cause.

[42] Prisoner Reentry: What Works, pp. 376-379.

[43] For more information about the use of randomized control trials to evaluate government programs, refer to CRS Report RL33301, *Congress and Program Evaluation: An Overview of Randomized Controlled Trials (RCTs) and Related Issues*, by Clinton T. Brass, Erin D. Williams, and Blas Nuñez-Neto.

[44] Questioning the Evidence, p. 7.

[45] Questioning the Evidence, pp. 6-7.

[46] Pamela K. Lattimore and Christy A. Visher, *The Multi-site Evaluation of SVORI: Summary and Synthesis*, RTI International, December 2009, http://svori.rti.org/documents/reports/SVORI_Summary_Synthesis_FINAL.pdf.

[47] The evaluation included a pre-release interview (conducted approximately 30 day before being released) with both SVORI and non-SVORI participants. Follow-up interviews were conducted 3, 9, and 15 months after release. In addition, oral swab drug tests were conducted during the 3 and 15 month interviews. Recidivism data was collected from the Federal Bureau of Investigation's National Crime Information Center (NCIC) and state correctional and juvenile justice agencies. Ibid., p. ES-7.

[48] A more detailed description of the Second Chance Act can be found in the **Appendix**.

[49] U.S. Department of Labor, Employment & Training Administration, "Serious and Violent Offender Reentry Initiative Appendices," available at http://www.doleta.gov/sga/sga/reentry_app.cfm.

[50] For more information about the Workforce Investment Act, please refer to CRS Report RL33687, *The Workforce Investment Act (WIA): Program-by-Program Overview and Funding of Title I Training Programs*, by David H. Bradley.

[51] For more information about the Work Opportunity Tax Credits Program, please refer to CRS Report RL30089, *The Work Opportunity Tax Credit (WOTC)*, by Christine Scott.

[52] U.S. Department of Labor, Employment & Training Administration, "Work Opportunity Tax Credit" available at http://www.doleta.gov/business/Incentives/opptax/.

[53] For more information about the Federal Bonding Program, please refer to CRS Report RL30248, *The Employment Service: The Federal-State Public Labor Exchange System*, by Alison Pasternak and Ann Lordeman.

[54] U.S. Department of Labor, Employment & Training Administration, "Federal Bonding Program," available at http://www.bonds4jobs.com/program-background.html.

[55] U.S. Department of Education, "Life Skills for State and Local Prisoners Program," available at http://www.ed.gov/programs/lifeskills/index.html.

[56] U.S. Department of Education, "Guide to U.S. Department of Education Programs, FY2007," p. 38, available at http://www.ed.gov/programs/gtep/gtep.pdf.

[57] U.S. Department of Labor, Employment & Training Administration, "Serious and Violent Offender Reentry Initiative Appendices," available at http://www.doleta.gov/sga/sga/reentry_app.cfm.

[58] U.S. Department of Labor, Employment & Training Administration, "Serious and Violent Offender Reentry Initiative Appendices," available at http://www.doleta.gov/sga/sga/reentry_app.cfm.

[59] For more information about SAMHSA, please refer to CRS Report RL33997, *Substance Abuse and Mental Health Services Administration (SAMHSA): Reauthorization Issues*, by Ramya Sundararaman (available by request).

[60] Testimony of Senior Policy Advisor to the Administrator Cheri Nolan, Substance Abuse and Mental Health Services Administration, U.S. Department of Health and Human Services, before the Committee on the Judiciary, Subcommittee on Corrections and Rehabilitation, Thursday, September 21, 2006.

[61] U.S. Department of Labor, Employment & Training Administration, "Serious and Violent Offender Reentry Initiative Appendices," available at http://www.doleta.gov/sga/sga/reentry_app.cfm.

[62] National Reentry Resource Center, *Federal Interagency Reentry Council*, http://www.nationalreentryresourcecenter.org/reentry-council.

[63] In order to be considered a "violent offender," an individual has to have committed this crime while in possession of a firearm or dangerous weapon, the crime has to have resulted in the death or serious bodily injury of a person, force had to have been used against someone's person, or the offender had 1 or more prior convictions for a felony crime of violence involving the use or attempted use of force against a person with the intent to cause death or serious bodily harm. See 42 U.S.C. 3797 u-2(a)(1).

[64] Pharmacological drug treatment involves using drugs and medications in the treatment of substance abuse. See Clayton Mosher, Scott Akins, and Chad Smith, "Pharmacological Drug Treatment" Paper presented at the annual meeting of the American Society of Criminology, Royal York, Toronto. 2008-04-21.

[65] States would be required to identify an entity that would be the single State administrative authority responsible for planning, developing, implementing, monitoring, regulating, and evaluating substance abuse services within the State.

[66] Grantees may exempt 10% of their clients from this 180-day requirement.

[67] 42 U.S.C. 15606(d)(3)(A).

In: Offender Reentry
Editor: Micah J. Hiram

ISBN: 978-1-63117-496-4
© 2014 Nova Science Publishers, Inc.

*Chapter 2*

# OFFENDER REENTRY ANNOTATED BIBLIOGRAPHY*

## *NIC Information Center*

## ABSTRACT

Each year, more than 700,000 individuals are released from state and federal prisons. Another 9 million cycle through local jails. When reentry fails, the costs—both societal and economic—are high. Because reentry intersects with issues of health and housing, education and employment, family, faith, and community well-being, many federal agencies are focusing on the reentry population with initiatives that aim to improve outcomes in each of these areas. This annotated bibliography addresses issues surrounding the reentry of offenders into the community. 135 entries are organized according to: reentry websites; reentry in general; reentry by category for community corrections, jails, prisons, community and family support, employment and housing, health and safety, and special populations; and reentry skills building.

---

* This is an edited, reformatted and augmented version of a document (Accession No. 026286) released by the National Institute of Corrections, dated July 2012 and revised January 2013.

# INTRODUCTION

Each year, more than 700,000 individuals are released from state and federal prisons.[1] Another 9 million cycle through local jails.[2] When reentry fails, the costs—both societal and economic—are high. Statistics indicate that more than two-thirds of state prisoners are rearrested within 3 years of their release and half are reincarcerated.[3] High rates of recidivism mean more crime, more victims, and more pressure on an already overburdened criminal justice system.

The costs of imprisonment also wreak havoc on state and municipal budgets. In the past 20 years state spending on corrections has grown at a faster rate than nearly any other state budget item. The U.S. now spends more than $68 billion on federal, state and local corrections.[4] Because reentry intersects with issues of health and housing, education and employment, family, faith, and community well-being, many federal agencies are focusing on the reentry population with initiatives that aim to improve outcomes in each of these areas.

Source: Federal Interagency Reentry Council

http://www. nationalreentryresourcecenter.org/reentry-council/activities

# REENTRY WEBSITES

*Alston Wilkes Society.* Last modified July 7, 2012. http://www. alstonwilkessociety.org.

The Alston Wilkes Society was founded in 1962 as a non-profit organization dedicated to providing rehabilitative services to adults released from correctional facilities. As an organization AWS extends a helping hand to those who are most at-risk and helps rebuild their lives through rehabilitation and prevention services. AWS was founded to provide services to adults who were being released from federal correctional facilities, and has grown to increase its service reach to include homeless veterans, at-risk families and disadvantaged and troubled youth.

*Bureau of Justice Assistance (BJA) Justice Today.* http://www.ojp.usdoj. gov/BJA/j_today/.

The BJA Justice Today newsletter contains information on BJA grant Funding and is a portal to various Federal partner activities and reports and to websites such as the Council for State Government. A recent newsletter included topics on innovative criminal justice practices, leadership development and training; reentry courts; and pretrial risk assessment. Justice Today also provides links to current news and various BJA publications including the BJA Annual report to Congress. Current and past issues of the newsletter are available online and future issues by subscription at

https://puborder.ncjrs.gov/listservs/subscribe_bjanewsletter.asp

*Community Oriented Policing.* http://www.cops.usdoj.gov/Default.asp? Item=2482.

The U.S. Department of Justice Community Oriented Policing website provides a unique window into the issue of reentry as it is focused on the role of law enforcement in offender reentry. It is a portal to papers on crime mapping, leadership, and law enforcement reentry strategies using "problem solving approaches", community policing, and collaborations with other agencies. The website also links to the PBS Frontline movie "Released" which is focused on mentally ill offenders returning to the community.

*Crimesolutions.gov.*          http://www.crimesolutions.gov/TopicDetails.aspx? ID=2.

You should go to this website first if you are looking for "[r]esearch on program effectiveness reviewed and rated by Expert Reviewers [with] [e]asily understandable ratings based on whether a program achieves its goals." Programs in the corrections and reentry field are divided into all, community corrections, inmate programs and treatment, recidivism, and reentry and release. In addition to corrections and reentry, the other broad topical areas are courts, crime and crime prevention, drugs and substance abuse, juveniles, law enforcement, technology and forensics, and victims and victimization.

*Dave Ramsey's Financial Peace University.* http://www.daveramsey.com/ correctional/home/.

Financial Peace University offers financial training designed to help offenders re-enter society. Too many offenders leave prison with little, if any, understanding of money management. This only makes it even more difficult for them to re-enter society with a solid foundation. Correctional institutions are beginning to combat this issue by offering Financial Peace University to offenders while they are in prison. As they learn the fundamentals of a healthy financial lifestyle, they become more equipped to manage their money when they leave the correctional facility—and less likely to return.

*Federal Interagency Reentry Council.* http://www.nationalreentry resourcecenter.org/reentry-Council.

In January 2011 Attorney General Eric Holder convened the inaugural meeting of the interagency Reentry Council. The purpose of this group is to bring together numerous federal agencies to make communities safer, assist those returning from prison and jail in becoming productive, tax-paying citizens, and save taxpayer dollars by lowering the direct and collateral costs of incarceration. Substantial commitments were made as result of the meeting. The Council also empowered staff—now representing 18 federal departments and agencies—to work towards a number of goals. And the Council agreed to meet every 6 months.

*Goodwill Industries International, Inc.* http://www.goodwill.org/ goodwill-for-you/specialized-services/people-with-criminal-backgrounds/.

This organization offers employment readiness training and job placement assistance. They believe that you can get a second chance. To begin, contact the Goodwill in your community and ask for an employment specialist. They understand that for people who have been incarcerated, there are many barriers to successful re-entry to public life, including drug dependency, serious illness, debt and limited work options. Just getting a second chance may seem almost impossible at times. They offer services to men, women and youth who have served their time and are trying to get back on track.

*International Association of Reentry.* http://www.iarreentry.org/ Home_Page.html.

The Mission of the Association is to foster community safety through the successful reintegration of offenders. This will be accomplished by promoting improved offender treatment and accountability, professional development and correctional reform. The IAR represents individuals, agencies and members who support prison population management, cost containment and successful reintegration of offenders in collaboration with those concerned with victims of crime, formerly incarcerated persons, correctional practitioners, allied justice professionals, higher education, public policy makers, inter-faith, family members and family advocates and community members.

"Justice Atlas of Sentencing and Corrections." *Justice Mapping Center.* Accessed July 9, 2012. http://www.justiceatlas.org.

"The Justice Atlas is a corrections data driven, interactive mapping tool ... [It] is distinct from crime mapping in that it maps the residential patterns of populations who are admitted to prison and who return to their communities from prison each year; as well as those who are on parole or probation on any typical day." Statistics are provided per state (if given) for admissions rate, count, and expenditure, releases rate, count, and expenditure, parole rate and count, and probation rate and count. Highlights from the data show revocations to prison, cost centers, reentry disparities, and gender rates.

*National Criminal Justice Initiatives Map.* *http://nicic.gov/Library/ 025224.* NY: National Reentry Resource Center, 2011.
Information about various reentry programs is provided via an interactive map of the United States. "The map, though not exhaustive, will seek to provide a place-based catalog of national initiatives and programs designed to reduce the recidivism rates of people returning from prison, jail, and juvenile facilities."

*National Reentry Resource Center.* http://www.nationalreentry resourcecenter.org. 2012. Sponsored by U.S. Bureau of Justice Assistance. The National Reentry Resource Center is the preeminent resource center for current research and policy reentry issues and publications. This website covers a full spectrum of topics and populations including juveniles, co-occurring (e.g., those with both substance abuse and mental health issues), physical health, housing, and victimization. It is both portal and library and provides an excellent source of reentry info including research reports; webinar announcements, conferences, funding opportunities, and news, has an upcoming events calendar and recently published the first Reentry myth-busters -- fact sheets generated by Federal agencies used to provide information about policies that impact offender reentry. The NRRC also has a Re-Entry Resource Map which provides state-by-state information on reentry efforts and publications catalogued according to audience. The affiliated Reentry Policy Council has a Reentry Programs Database where you can search by topic or by state. The monthly newsletter is available for subscription and past issues are available on-line. Archived Webcasts are listed at http://www.nationalreentryresourcecenter.org/training/webcasts.

*The Next Step: Cooperative of Felon Friendly Employers.* https://www. thenextstep99.com/.

The Next Step brings together recently released Federal and State Felons (Candidates) looking for work, the Agencies and Facilities that manage their post-release experience, and "Felon-Friendly" Employers who appreciate the value these men and women can bring to the workplace. We manage the "Coffee" database -- the Cooperative of Felon Friendly Employers. This is the most comprehensive nationwide network of employers willing to hire ex-felons.

*Office of Justice Programs Reentry Initiative.* https://www.bja.gov/ ProgramDetails.aspx?Program_ID The Reentry Initiative is supported by the U.S. Department of Justice's Office of Justice Programs (OJP) and its federal partners: the U.S. Departments of Education, Health and Human Services, Housing and Urban Development, and Labor. This initiative is a comprehensive effort that addresses both juvenile and adult populations of serious, high-risk offenders. It provides funding to develop, implement, enhance, and evaluate reentry strategies that will ensure the safety of the community and the reduction of serious, violent crime. This is accomplished by preparing targeted offenders to successfully return to their communities after having served a significant period of secure confinement in a state training school, juvenile or adult correctional facility, or other secure institution.

*Prisoner Reentry Institute.* http://www.jjay.cuny.edu/centers/prisoner_ reentry_institute/2704.htm.

John Jay College of Criminal Justice. Prisoner Reentry Institute (New York, NY)

This website will be a valuable resource for those people interested in effectiveness of reentry procedures and practices. Points of entry include: about PRI; current initiatives; occasional series events; publications/resources; contact information; and institute spotlights.

"Reentry." *Center for Effective Public Policy,* last modified July 9, 2012. http://cepp.com/reentry.

Even as offenders transition to the community, a significant proportion of them return from the community to prison in fairly short order for new crimes or for violations of parole. As a result, in recent years, the correctional community has begun to focus on the challenge of helping a growing number of offenders make a safe transition from prison to the community. The Center for Effective Public Policy is committed to working with agencies around the country to bolster their efforts to not only maintain safe and secure institutions and encourage effective supervision practices, but also to equip offenders during and after their incarceration to be law-abiding once released. To this end, the Center has worked with dozens of jurisdictions on transition issues and has developed a number of written models, products, and curricula aimed at building staff and agency capacity to support successful reentry practices.

*Reentry Into Society.* http://www.nij.gov/nij/topics/corrections/reentry/welcome.htm.

National Institute of Justice (NIJ) reentry efforts are highlighted on this website. This website begins with an overview of prisoner reentry, a discussion of the need for coordinated reentry services, and a brief look at the NIJ's reentry research portfolio. Additional links on the site are: evaluation of the Serious and Violent Offender Reentry Initiative (SVORI); evaluation of Second Chance Act Demonstration Projects; research on reentry and employment; publications on reentry, parole, and probation; related content about community corrections and recidivism; reentry trends in the U.S.; and audiovisual resources.

*Reentry Policy Council.* http://justicecenter.csg.org. A project of the Council of State Governments Justice Center. The Reentry Policy Council (RPC) was established in 2001 to assist state government officials grappling with the increasing number of people leaving prisons and jails to return to the communities they left behind. The RPC was formed with two specific goals in mind: To develop bipartisan policies and principles for elected officials and other policymakers to consider as they evaluate reentry issues in their jurisdictions. To facilitate coordination and information-sharing among organizations implementing reentry initiatives, researching trends, communicating about related issues, or funding projects.

*Resource Directory for Prisoners.* http://www.naljorprisondharmaservice.org/resourcedirectory.htm

Guide for enabling inmates to connect with various outreach and personal growth services. These programs are organized into the following areas: spiritual resources—Buddhist; spiritual resources—Christian; spiritual resources—Hindu and Yoga; further resources for psychological and spiritual transformation—ageless wisdom, interfaith, metaphysical, Native American, and psychology; legal support; free book resources; pen pal correspondence— Buddhist, Christian, Jewish, and non-religious; creative writing, artistic resources, newsletters, and magazines; reentry assistance, and family and personal support; jobs, careers, and continuing education; personal health and nutrition; and a few things to think about if you are incarcerated.

*Safer Foundation.* http://www.saferfoundation.org/news-views/other-documents-of-interest.

Safer's mission is to reduce recidivism by supporting, through a full spectrum of services, the efforts of people with criminal records to become employed, law-abiding members of the community. Safer's post-release employment and educational services include supportive services, retention services, market cultivation, youth empowerment programs, faith- and community based initiatives and housing initiatives.

*Urban Institute.* http://www.urban.org/justice/corrections.cfm.

The Urban Institute is a first rate research and public policy organization. The Justice Policy Center focuses on the full spectrum of the criminal justice system, but of particular note is Urban's work in the areas of offender re-entry from prison and jail; research on serious violent offenders (SVORI) and their focus on conducting cost-benefit analyses of various initiatives. In addition, Urban has advanced our understanding of crime mapping and continues to push the field forward in the areas of the role of family on reentry and the impact of offending on children and communities and houses the Federal Justice Statistics Resource Center. The Justice Policy Center (JPC) website has a library containing updated research on these and many other topics and the JPC Reentry newsletter, published monthly, contains links to recent presentations, publications and news related to the Urban Institute. The newsletter is available through a list-serve; contact jpcgeneral@lists.urban.org.

*What Works in Reentry Clearinghouse.* http://nationalreentry resourcecenter.org/what_works.

This website provides access to research on the effectiveness of reentry programs and practices for practitioners and service providers seeking guidance on evidence-based reentry interventions. It is also a useful resource for researchers and others interested in reentry. Focus areas include brand name programs, employment, housing, and mental health. Other focus areas coming soon, so you want to keep checking back. Other points of entry to this site include: about the center; training and technical assistance; library; reentry facts; what works; and tools and resources.

# REENTRY – GENERAL

*Advancing Practice: Experimentation, Implementation, Sustainability - Spotlight on Reentry*. Fairfax, VA: George Mason University, Center for Advancing Correctional Excellence, 2012.

This edition looks at the ongoing work of the Center for Advancing Correctional Excellence (ACE) related to prisoner reentry. Articles in this issue include: "An Introduction by ACE Director Fay S. Taxman"; "EMTAP: Evidence Mapping to Advance Justice Practice" by Jennifer Lerch; "Corrections Officers' Role in Reentry" by Lerch; "Mental Health Issues in Reentry" by Carolyn Watson; "Probation & Parole: Uncovering What Works with Still a lot to Learn!" by Danielle S. Rudes; "Hearing from the Experts: A Practitioner, a Participant, and a Professor [Kari Galloway, Lars Peterson, and Joan Petersilia]" by Rudes; "Reentry Checklist" by Taxman; and "Reentry: Collaboration is Key" by Taxman.

http://nicic.gov/Library/026037

Baer, Demelza, *et al. Understanding the Challenges of Prisoner Reentry: Research Findings from the Urban Institute's Prisoner Reentry Portfolio*. Washington, DC: Urban Institute, Justice Policy Center, 2006.

Research conducted and reported by the Urban Institute regarding prisoner reentry is highlighted. Results are organized into the following areas: employment and reentry; health and reentry; housing and reentry; substance use and reentry; families and reentry; communities and reentry; public safety and reentry; community supervision and reentry; strategic partnerships and collaboration; and select prisoner reentry publications as of January 2006.

http://www.urban.org/UploadedPDF/411289_reentry_portfolio.pdf

*Coaching Packet Series 1-3*. Washington, DC: Center for Effective Public Policy, 2010.

Each of these Coaching Packets provides an overview of a key topic related to successful offender reentry, concrete strategies and key steps for enhancing practice in this area, and a "self assessment tool" that jurisdictions can use to evaluate their strengths and challenges in the particular topic area discussed." "Coaching Packet Series 1: Creating a Blueprint for an Effective Offender Reentry System" includes "A Framework for Offender Reentry," "Establishing a Rational Planning Process," and "Engaging in Collaborative Partnerships to Support Reentry." "Coaching Packet Series 2: Delivering Evidence-Based Services" has "Implementing Evidence-Based Practices,"

"Effective Case Management," "Shaping Offender Behavior," "Engaging Offenders' Families in Reentry," "Building Offenders' Community Assets Through Mentoring," and "Reentry Considerations for Women Offenders." "Coaching Packet Series 3: Ensuring Meaningful Outcomes" contains "Measuring the Impact of Reentry Efforts" and "Continuous Quality Improvement."

http://cepp.com/documents/Center-for-Effective-Public-Policy-Coaching-Packets.pdf

*Employing Your Mission: Building Cultural Competence in Reentry Service Agencies Through the Hiring of Individuals Who Are Formerly Incarcerated and/or in Recovery.* Washington, DC: U.S. Bureau of Justice Assistance, 2011.

This publication will be useful to those individuals wanting to make their reentry services more effective. The building of cultural competence "within reentry services by hiring formerly incarcerated men and women to reflect the experiences and realities of the reentry population and provide services more effectively" is explained (p. 1). Cultural competence is a set of practices that work to make an organization more successful in cross-cultural conditions. Four sections in addition to a summary are contained in this Toolkit: research literature review; case study—how the Fortune Society builds cultural competence through hiring and management practices; the Thames Reach story--applying the Fortune Society's cultural competence hiring strategies to other organizations; and getting started today--developing cultural competence through hiring and department practice.

http://fortunesociety.org/wp-content/uploads/TOOL-KIT-2_Employing-Your-Mission_FINAL-Lo-Res-Emailable_110501.pdf

*A Framework for Evidence-Based Decision Making in Local Criminal Justice Systems,* 3rd ed.
Washington, DC: Center for Effective Public Policy, 2010.

This report is essential reading for individuals wanting to achieve "measurable reductions of pretrial misconduct and post-conviction reoffending" (p.6). Eight sections follow an introduction (a new paradigm for the justice system): underlying premises; the key decision points, decision makers, and stakeholders in the criminal justice system; examining justice system decision making through the lens of harm reduction; the principles underlying the framework; applying evidence-based principles to practice; key

challenges to implementing this framework; collaboration—a key ingredient of an evidence-based system; and building evidence-based agencies.
   http://nicic.gov/Library/024372

Gideon, Lior, and Hung-En Sung, eds. *Rethinking Corrections: Rehabilitation, Reentry, and Reintegration.* Thousand Oaks, CA: Sage Publications, 2011.

This book explores challenges experienced by offenders during rehabilitation and reintegration and relevant policy implications. Chapters include: "Corrections in the Era of Reentry" by Lior Gideon; "Public Attitudes Toward Rehabilitation and Reintegration: How Supportive Are People of Getting-Tough-on-Crime Policies and the Second Chance Act?" by Gideon and Natalie Loveland; "Treatment of Offender Populations: Implications for Risk Management and Community Reintegration" by Elizabeth L. Jeglic, Christian Maile, and Cynthia Calkins-Mercado; "Major Rehabilitative Approaches" by Hung-En Sung and Gideon; "Probation: An Untapped Resource in U.S. Corrections" by Doris Layton MacKenzie; "Diversion Programs" by Rachel Porter; "Prison-Based Substance Abuse Programs" by Wayne N. Welsh; "Prison-Based Educational and Vocational Training Programs" by Georgen Guerrero; "Community Reintegration of Violent and Sexual Offenders: Issues and Challenges for Community Risk Management" by Patrick Lussier, Melissa Dahabieh, Nadine Deslauriers-Varin, and Chris Thomson; "Seeking Medical and Psychiatric Attention" by Elizabeth Corzine McMullan; "Faith-Based Prisoner Reentry" by Beverly D. Frazier; "Parole: Moving the Field Forward Through a New Model of Behavioral Management" by Faye S. Taxman; "Employment Barriers to Reintegration" by Mindy S. Tarlow; "Barriers to Reintegration" by Andrea Leverentz; "Rehabilitation, Reentry, and Reintegration in Criminal Justice Education" by Gideon; and "Conclusion: Integrative Triple R Theory: Rehabilitation, Reentry, and Reintegration" by Gideon and Sung.

Gnall, Kathleen. *Learning From People Who Succeed Upon Release: Strategies, Approaches and Tools That Can Make a Difference.* NY: National Reentry Resource Center, 2012.

"Suggestions for adopting organizational strategies [for offender reentry programs] informed by evaluation findings, practitioners, and those who have transitioned successfully" (p. 5). Topics discussed during this presentation include: reasons to be optimistic regarding the criminal justice system; what we can do better and we are committed to doing so; an expert's viewpoint;

moving forward; context for change; selection of successful strategies; what
we are asking of the offender; individual change is difficult, but not
impossible; supporting positive change; the Risk-Needs-Responsivity RNR)
Model; other tools; lessons from ex-offenders; family, strength-based
approach; what offenders say they need; community factors; and concluding
suggestions. http://nicic.gov/Library/026515

Immarigeon, Russ, and Larry M. Fehr, eds. *Pathways for Offender
Reentry: An ACA Reader.* Alexandria, VA: American Correctional
Association, 2012.
   "The articles in this book profile advances in reentry research, policy, and
practice. They reflect the state of the art in correctional reentry from federal,
state, and local correctional systems... (p. xv). Twenty-one articles are
organized into six parts: prisoner reentry; building prisoner reentry through
collaborative partnerships; successful reentry work; what makes reentry work;
future perspective regarding offender reintegration; and further resources.
Some of the topics covered include: a new era in prisoner reentry; barriers due
to criminal records; reintegration efforts with female offenders; challenges and
opportunities for collaborative partnerships; reentry efforts in Ohio; the
challenges of successful reentry; the experience of San Diego; parole
supervision strategies to enhance reentry outcomes; family-focused justice
reform; fathers and families; evidence-based practices in the integration of
criminal justice and recovery-oriented systems of care; increasing employment
opportunities in California; collaborative solutions for reentry housing; the
potential of reintegrative justice; the challenge of pragmatic solutions; and
restorative justice. Copyrighted.

La Vigne, Nancy, *et al. Release Planning for Successful Reentry: A Guide
for Corrections, Service Providers, and Community Groups.* Washington, DC:
Urban Institute, Justice Policy Center, 2008.
   "The purpose of this report is to describe the specific elements that
together embody thoughtful and effective prisoner release procedures" (p. 4).
Sections following an executive summary are: introduction; what release
planning is; what the key components of a release plan are; what the
opportunities and challenges of release planning are; and conclusion.
   http://nicic.gov/Library/023334

Meyers-Peeples, Roberta, and April L. Frazier. *National Blueprint for
Reentry: Model Policies to Promote the Successful Reentry of Individuals with*

*Criminal Records through Employment and Education.* New York: Legal Action Center, National H.I.R.E. Network, 2008.

The National Blueprint for Reentry, "a comprehensive plan for developing a national policy agenda to improve employment and educational opportunities for people with criminal records" is provided (p. 2). Sections of this report include: executive summary; introduction; education background and recommendations; employment background and recommendations; conclusion; state and local model policies; and copies of presentation overheads for "Becoming a Powerful Advocate in Washington, DC: Mastering the Federal Advocacy Process."

http://nicic.gov/Library/023501

*Office of Justice Programs' Management of Its Offender Reentry Initiatives.* Washington, DC: U.S. Department of Justice, Office of the Inspector General, Audit Division, 2010.

Results from an evaluation of the Office of Justice Programs' two major offender reentry initiatives are presented and analyzed. Sections following an executive summary are: introduction; findings and recommendations regarding the administration and management of OJP's offender reentry programs and design of OJP's offender reentry grant programs; Statement of Compliance with Laws and Regulations; and Statement on Internal Controls. Appendixes also provide a response from the OJP and the OIG Analysis and Summary of Actions Necessary to Close the Report. "OJP did not establish an effective system for monitoring the SVORI [Serious and Violent Offender Reentry Initiative] and PRI [Prisoner Reentry Initiative] grantees to assess whether they were meeting program goals" and had "significant design flaws in the initial implementation" of these programs (p.ii).

http://nicic.gov/Library/024581

*Reentry MythBusters.* Washington, DC: National Reentry Resource Center, Federal Interagency Reentry Council. Accessed 9 July, 2012.

Reentry Myth Busters are a series of "fact sheets intended to clarify existing federal policies that affect formerly incarcerated individuals and their families." Topics covered are: formalized processes for reducing child support orders during incarceration; social security benefit reinstatement; exceptions to termination of parental rights while incarcerated; the Federal Bonding Program (FBP); Temporary Assistance for Needy Families (TANF) and welfare bans; federal student financial aid; Supplemental Nutrition Assistance Program (SNAP, formerly Food Stamp Program); criminal records and barred employment; Criminal records and Federal Government employment; SNAP benefits and a valid state ID; SNAP and a mailing address; resumption of Veterans Administration (VA) benefits; and public housing. http://www. nationalreentryresourcecenter.org/documents/0000/1090/REENTRY_MYTHB USTERS.pdf

*Report of the Re-Entry Policy Council: Charting the Safe and Successful Return of Prisoners to the Community.* Washington, DC: Reentry Policy Council, 2005.

Policy statements, "each of which is a consensus-based principle that should be the underpinning of a re-entry initiative," are presented (p. xix). These 35 statements are organized into the following areas: getting started; addressing core challenges; admission to the facility; prison- and jail-based programming; making the release decision; managing the key transition period; community supervision; and elements of effective social service systems. Appendixes provide: information about programs cited as examples in this report; a chart of status of parole by state; an explanation of justice mapping; voting restrictions for people with felony convictions; and a glossary.

   http://nicic.gov/Library/020211

Severson, Margaret E., *et al.* "Who Goes Back to Prison; Who Does Not: A Multiyear View of Reentry Program Participants." *Journal of Offender Rehabilitation,* 51:5, 295-315, 2012.

Existing studies of reentry programs in the United States focus on the successes and failures of reentering offenders when compared to matched reentering offenders who did not receive structured reentry services. Little attention has been focused solely on the reentry participants themselves, and on how the level of program exposure may be related to recidivism outcomes. This study reports the recidivism outcomes of 357 reentry participants released to the community during a multiyear study period. All of the 357 participants studied were released for at least one full year, making it possible to examine recidivism behaviors by levels of reentry program exposure, at similar points in time. Thus, a range of descriptive and program attributes and an analysis of these attributes vis-a`-vis defined recidivism measures is presented to answer the question: ''Who goes back to prison?''

   http://dx.doi.org/10.1080/10509674.2012.677944

Wilkinson, Reginald A., ed. *Reentry Best Practices: Directors' Perspectives.* Middletown, CT: Association of State Correctional Administrators, 2004.

This document "highlight[s] outstanding initiatives and programs associated with the growing national movement in corrections targeting offender reentry" (p. v). Eighty-six articles are organized into five chapters: prison programs; transitional programs; mental health and substance abuse programs; community and supervision strategies; and promising or unique services.

http://www.asca.net/system/assets/attachments/891/Reentry_Best_Practice s_Publication.pdf?1280168375

# REENTRY - COMMUNITY CORRECTIONS

Ball, David, Robert Weisberg, and Kara Dansky. *The First 72 Hours of Re-Entry: Seizing the Moment of Release.* Stanford, CA: Stanford Criminal Justice Center, 2008.

The importance of the first 72 hours of release from a correctional facility for successful parolee reentry is explained. Sections following an executive summary are: introduction; pre-release planning in prison; focus -- the first 72 hours; choreographing the first 72 hours; the larger lessons of the first 72 hours; and conclusion -- the first 72 hours revisited. http://nicic.gov/ Library/023646

Bartruff, Jerry, Nathan Lowe, and Shawn Rogers. *Webinar: Evidence-Based Practices of Community Supervision: Part 2, What Works in Parole and the Prisoner Reentry Process.* New York: National Reentry Resource Center, 2011.

"The goal of this webinar is to educate community corrections professionals on evidence-based practices of parole supervision, particularly with respect to the reentry of parolees leaving prison." Participants will be able to: understand the core elements of EBPs and parole supervision; discuss the pros and cons of EBPs implementation; recognize leadership qualities that are conducive to using a successful evidence-based approach; and identify at least two practices that they could implement to enhance parole supervision and reentry outcomes.

http://nicic.gov/Library/025517

Burke, Peggy, and Michael Tonry. *Successful Transition and Reentry for Safer Communities: A Call to Action for Parole.* Silver Spring, MD: Center for Effective Public Policy, 2006.

The critical role of paroling authorities and parole supervision agencies in the successful reintegration of offenders into the community is explained. Sections of this report are: introduction; successful reentry as community safety -- the significant consequences of unsuccessful reentry; what we know about success -- putting the lessons of research into practice; parole in 2006 -- a century of evolution (e.g., the rehabilitative ideal, just deserts, deterrence and incapacitation, parole's decline, lessons of experience, and readiness and tools for change; and an agenda for action.

http://www.cepp.com/documents/A%20Call%20to%20Action%20for%20Parole.pdf

Guevara, Meghan, and Enver Solomon. *Implementing Evidence-Based Policy and Practice in Community Corrections:* 2nd ed. Washington, DC: National Institute of Corrections, 2009.

A "guide for [community corrections] agencies to transform themselves into evidence-based organizations" is provided (p.xv). Six chapters follow an executive summary: what evidence-based practice is; the integrated model; the principles of effective intervention; implementing evidence-based principles; leading organizational change and development; and collaboration for systemic change. The appendixes include: research support gradient; the search conference; and key concepts in organizational development.

http://nicic.gov/Downloads/PDF/Library/024107.pdf

Hamilton, Zachary. *Do Reentry Courts Reduce Recidivism? Results from the Harlem Parole Reentry Court.* New York: Center for Court Innovation, 2010.

Those wanting to implement a reentry court in their community can use this report to show how such courts greatly benefit public safety. Six chapters follow an executive summary: introduction; the state of prisoner reentry; the reentry court model; study design and analysis plan; results according to recidivism and reincarceration rates, months to rearrest/revocation, role of duration, and predictors of completion/graduation (prior behavior seems to indicate future behavior); and discussion and conclusion. "The findings indicate that the Reentry Court program has a positive impact with regard to preventing new criminal behavior—rearrests and revocations" (p.29).

http://nicic.gov/Library/024350

Lucht, Jim, Nancy G. La Vigne, and Megan Denver. *Enhancing Supervision and Support for Released Prisoners: A Documentation and Evaluation of the Community Supervision Mapping System.* Washington, DC: National Institute of Justice, 2011.

The "Community Supervision Mapping System (CSMS), an online tool that enables users to map the formerly incarcerated and others on probation, along with related data such as service provider locations and police districts" is described (p. v). Agencies looking to design and implement such a system should read this article. It will provide you with valuable information for getting your project off the ground. Sections of this report following an executive summary include: introduction; concept and theoretical framework; CSMS project background; development; implementation; evaluation findings regarding CSMS users, CSMS visits and patterns of use, frequency of use, most commonly used CSMS features, user perceptions of CSMS, user focus groups, other interviews, and summary; looking forward; and conclusion.

http://nicic.gov/Library/026396

Morgan, Robert D., Daryl G. Kroner, and Jeremy F. Mills. *Re-entry: Dynamic Risk Assessment.* Technical Report. Washington, DC: National Institute of Justice, 2011.

This study aims to examine the dynamic predictors of post-release outcomes for parolees reentering the community. Sections of this report following an abstract are: executive summary; technical report—introduction, methods, and results; and conclusions. "Most notably, in this study changes in offenders dynamic functioning was not associated with changes in community outcomes. That is, measuring change in offenders functioning using rated measures did not increase our ability to predict community failure. More Importantly however, offenders were able to self-report risk areas that were predictive of community failure suggesting that offenders should be involved in the criminal risk assessment" (p. 3).

http://nicic.gov/Library/026040

*Parole, Desistance from Crime, and Community Integration.* Washington, DC: National Research Council, Division of Behavioral and Social Sciences and Education, Committee on Law and Justice, 2008.

Individuals should turn to this book if they want to know what is known "about various models of community supervision designed to reduce recidivism and promote desistance from crime" (p. ix). Sections following an executive summary include: introduction and background; dimensions of desistance; parole-current practices; services and practices for releases; criminal justice institutions and community resources; and conclusions, recommendations, and research agenda. It seems that recidivism is greatly reduced through the use of cognitive-treatment programs.

http://www.nap.edu/catalog.php?record_id=11988&utm_campaign=AddT his&utm_source=email&utm_medium=share#.T0xoqZWqR3o.email

Petersilia, Joan. *When Prisoners Come Home: Parole and Prisoner Reentry*. New York: Oxford University Press, 2003.

The "systems, people, programs, and prospects for implementing a more effective and just [prisoner reentry] system" are analyzed (p. vi). The ten chapters comprising this book are: the emerging importance of prisoner reentry to crime and community; a profile of returning prisoners; the origins and evolution of modern parole; the changing nature of parole supervision and services; preparing inmates for release; legal and practical barriers to reintegration; inmate release and recidivism -- revolving door justice; the victim's role in prisoner reentry; reforming parole and reentry practices; and when punitive policies backfire.

Rudes, Danielle S., Jennifer Lerch, and Faye S. Taxman. "Implementing a Reentry Framework at a Correctional Facility: Challenges to the Culture." *Journal of Offender Rehabilitation*, 50:8, 467-491, 2011.

Implementation research is emerging in the field of corrections, but few studies have examined the complexities associated with implementing change among frontline workers embedded in specific organizational cultures. Using a mixed methods approach, the authors examine the challenges faced by correctional workers in a work release correctional facility during their transformation into a reentry center. Findings reveal that staff report a low readiness for change while observational and interview data confirm that staff attitudes and accompanying behaviors undermine efforts to provide a humane environment for reentry. This study illustrates the value of using quantitative and qualitative methods to understand and measure key organizational issues that affect the ability to alter the milieu for delivering services. The authors examine how inertia regarding reforms is not due to the nature of the reform but rather to the culture of the organization and how important it is to address organizational culture. They also highlight the importance of integrating interactional and routine practices among frontline workers as part of a strategy to reform correctional facilities.

http://dx.doi.org/10.1080/10509674.2011.624392

Solomon, Amy L., *et al. Putting Public Safety First -- 13 Parole Supervision Strategies to Enhance Reentry Outcomes.* Washington, DC: Urban Institute, Justice Policy Center, 2008.

Organization-level and individual-level strategies for improving the supervision of offenders in the community are described. Sections of this report include: introduction -- background and focus of this paper; define success as recidivism reduction and measure performance; tailor conditions of supervision; focus resources on moderate and high-risk parolees; front-load supervision resources; implement earned discharge; implement place-based supervision; engage partners to expand intervention capacities; assess criminogenic risk and need factors; develop and implement supervision case plans that balance surveillance and treatment; involve parolees to enhance their engagement in assessment, case planning, and supervision; engage informal social controls to facilitate community reintegration; incorporate incentives and rewards into the supervision process; employ graduated problem-solving responses to violations of parole conditions in a swift and certain manner; and repositioning parole supervision -- looking ahead.

http://nicic.gov/Library/023433

Wolf, Robert V. *Reentry Courts: Looking Ahead: A Conversation about Strategies for Offender Reintegration.* New York: Center for Court Innovation, 2011.

Anyone interested in reentry courts will find this report's insights informative. Topics discussed include current research, key program elements, eligibility requirements, managing the transition from prison to reentry court, evidence-based practices, adapting the drug court model, developing support for reentry initiatives, statewide coordination of reentry courts, overcoming institutional divisions, funding, and composition of the reentry court team.

http://nicic.gov/Library/025081

# REENTRY – JAILS

Carmody, Justin. *Effective County Practices in Jail to Community Transition Planning for Offenders with Mental Health and Substance Abuse Disorders.* Washington, DC: National Association of Counties, Community Services Division, 2008.

This publication focuses on defining the essential components of effective transition planning for this population [of inmates with co-occurring disorders] and showcases studies of promising county practices from across the country. Sections of this report include: introduction; components of effective transition planning; six model programs; Allegheny County (PA); Auglaize County; Black Hawk County (IA); Macomb County (MI); Montgomery County (MD); and Multnomah County.

    http://nicic.gov/Library/023440


Christensen, Gary E. *Our System of Corrections: Do Jails Play a Role in Improving Offender Outcomes?* Washington, DC: National Institute of Corrections, Community Corrections Division, 2008.

"This document will review the role of jails and incarceration within United States' correctional systems and propose opportunities for jail officials to interact and collaborate with local criminal justice entities with the shared purpose of enhancing long-term public safety" (p. ix). Sections following an abstract include: practice within corrections -- does it work as a system; corrections within the U.S.—the current context; evidence-based practice -- the effectiveness of criminal sanctions; communicating within a social learning environment; offender classification -- to jail or not to jail; the work of jails—high-risk offenders and their effect on public safety; organizational/system change—the role of correctional leadership; high-risk offenders in jail transition programs; and conclusion/summary. Appendixes include: "An Example of a Successful Jail Transition Program: The Dutchess County Jail Transition Program [DCJTP]"; DCJTP 5-Week Plan—Checklist; and DCJTP Plan for Transition form.

    http://nicic.gov/Library/023357


*Jail Reentry Roundtable Initiative.* Washington, DC: Urban Institute, Justice Policy Center, 2006.

A digest of presentations and discussions regarding the reentry of jail inmates is supplied. Thirteen sections comprise this document: introduction and meeting overview; what we know about jails at the national level; inmate challenges; the NCCD-Zogby poll regarding public attitudes toward rehabilitation and reentry -- findings; short-term interventions; the role of community supervision in addressing reentry from jails; what recidivism entails; evidence-based reentry practices in the jail setting; reentry from jails for females; the economics of jail reentry; jail/community linkages; reentry from rural jails; and final comments and next steps.

    http://www.urban.org/url.cfm?ID=411368

Jannetta, Jesse, Hannah Dodd, and Brian Elderbroom. *The Elected Official's Toolkit for Jail Reentry.*
Washington, DC: Urban Institute, Justice Policy Center, 2011.

Those individuals involved in creating a jail reentry program will find this publication very useful. Information about various issues related to jail reentry is provided on single topic handouts. These handouts are divided into two sections--fact sheets regarding jail reentry and its key components and tools and resources for implementing or expanding a jail reentry initiative.
http://nicic.gov/Library/024845

Mellow, Jeff, *et al. The Jail Administrator's Toolkit for Reentry.* Washington, DC: Urban Institute, Justice Policy Center, 2008.

Guidance is provided for preparing inmates for their transition from jail to the community. This Toolkit contains these sections: getting started; jail staff issues; assessment screens; reentry strategies; identifying community resources; coordinating stakeholders and educating the public; requirements and standards; measuring success; and conclusion. Copies of pertinent forms are also included.
http://nicic.gov/Library/023068

Solomon, Amy L., *et al. Life After Lockup: Improving Reentry from Jail to the Community.* Washington, DC: Urban Institute, Justice Policy Center, 2008.

Lessons learned by the Jail Reentry Roundtable Initiative are shared. This report is divided into five sections: facts about U.S. jails and the jail population; addressing reentry from jails -- making the most of a short stay; examples from the field; the role of probation in reentry from jail; and looking forward.
http://nicic.gov/Library/023067

*Transition from Jail to Community Online Learning Toolkit.* Washington, DC: National Institute of Corrections, 2010.

This online learning resource is an essential ingredient in the development of programs designed to help offenders reenter the community upon their release from jail. This program contains the following nine modules: getting started; leadership, vision, and organizational culture; collaborative structure and joint ownership; data-driven understanding of local reentry; targeted intervention strategies; screening and assessment; transition plan development; targeted transition interventions; and self-evaluation and sustainability.

http://nicic.gov/Library/024369

## REENTRY – PRISONS

Boehm, Julie. *Missouri Reentry Process.* Jefferson City, MO: Missouri Dept. of Corrections, 2007. The use of the National Institute of Corrections' Transition from Prison to Community Initiative (TPCI) by the Missouri Department of Corrections is briefly explained. "The TPCI model offers Missouri a framework, process and set of principles for a system wide approach to preparing offenders for success in the community" (p. 1). Links at this website related to the Missouri Reentry Process (MRP) include a quarterly newsletter, MRP flowchart, MRP principles, and a transitional accountability plan brochure.
    http://doc.mo.gov/mrp/mrp.php

Burke, Peggy B., *et al. TPC Case Management Handbook: An Integrated Case Management Approach.* Washington, DC: National Institute of Corrections, 2010.
    Designed for teams of correctional and non-correctional staff at policy, management, and line staff levels who have been charged with implementing improvements in supervision and case management that support an overall strategy to reduce recidivism and enhance community safety through successful offender reentry. Chapters include: an overview of the Integrated Case Management approach; critical challenges and strengths of the ICM approach; roles and responsibilities of staff; implementation strategy for agencies committing to ICM; and a final word on organizational and cultural change.
    http://nicic.gov/Library/024393

Burke, Peggy B. *TPC Reentry Handbook: Implementing the NIC Transition from Prison to the Community Model.* Silver Spring, MD: Center for Effective Public Policy, 2008. Developed for a broad range of stakeholders involved in improving reentry practices. Chapters include: transition and reentry—a key public policy issue; the Transition from Prison to the Community (TPC) model; why and how to take on the challenge of transition and reentry—lessons from the eight TPC states; implementing the TPC model; case management—a critical element of the TPC model; TPC performance measurement framework; and emerging issues, challenges, and opportunities.

Appendixes include: capsule descriptions of TPC implementation in the eight pilot states; and examples from the implementation efforts of these states— forming and chartering teams, articulating a vision, documenting current population, policy, and practice, improving the use of information, evidence- based practice, identifying targets of change and setting priorities, improving offender management, preparing organizations for change, case management, and emerging issues, challenges, and opportunities.

http://nicic.gov/Library/022669

Carter, Madeline M., ed. *Increasing Public Safety through Successful Offender Reentry: Evidence-Based and Emerging Practices in Corrections.* Silver Spring, MD: Center for Effective Public Policy, 2007.

The implementation of an effective offender reentry framework is explained. Sections contained in this manual include: introduction; offender reentry from a national perspective; framework for offender reentry; leadership and organizational change; a rational planning process for a learning organization; the essential role of collaboration; key strategies in effective offender management; women offenders; and conclusion. Also provided is a copy of the Offender Reentry Policy and Practice Inventory.

http://nicic.gov/Library/023247

*The Federal Bureau of Prisons Inmate Release Preparation and Transitional Reentry Programs.* Washington, DC: U.S. Department of Justice, Office of the Inspector General, Audit Division, 2004.

The ability of the BOP to ensure "that federal inmates participate in its programs designed to prepare them for successful reentry into society" is evaluated (p. ii). Sections of this report are: executive summary; introduction; incarceration and recidivism statistics; BOP reentry programs; release planning; Inmate Skills Development Re-engineering Initiative; and findings and recommendations regarding reentry program completions and Community Corrections Centers.

http://www.usdoj.gov/oig/reports/BOP/a0416/index.htm

*Final Report of the* [Florida] *Governor's Ex-Offender Task Force.* Baltimore, MD: Annie E. Casey Foundation, 2006.

Recommendations for making the process of ex-offender reentry more effective in Florida are presented. This report contains these sections: executive summary; introduction; the prison experience -- successful reentry must start at prison entry; coming home -- reentry at the community level; and organizing reentry reform work in 2007 and beyond.

http://www.aecf.org/KnowledgeCenter/Publications.aspx?pubguid=%7BF 545D6BE-4DB7-4518-B85D-7536364CA20B%7D

Haas, Stephen M., Cynthia A. Hamilton, and Dena Hanley. *Preparing Prisoners for Returning Home: A Process Evaluation of West Virginia's Offender Reentry Initiative.* Charleston, WV: Mountain State Criminal Justice Research Services, 2007.

Pre-release programs provided to soon-to-be-released inmates are evaluated. This report contains these sections: executive summary; introduction; present analysis; results for pre-release programs provided to inmates, program delivery and length of time served, institutional programs provided, transitional programs provided, and prisoner needs and treatment matching; and key findings and evidence-based recommendations for the Offender Reentry Initiative overall. Appendixes include: Individual Reentry Program Plan; Program Recommendation Matrix; Parole Release Plan form; Aftercare Plan form; and program categories and descriptions.

http://www.ojp.usdoj.gov/BJA/evaluation/program-corrections/reentry6. htm

Johnson, Byron. *Not by Government Nor Faith Alone: Rethinking Prisoner Reentry.* Washington, DC: Department of Health and Human Services, Center for Faith-Based and Community Initiatives, 2008.

This paper "reviews research documenting the role of religion in prisons and prisoner reentry, and reviews research connecting religion to crime reduction as well as prosocial behavior, and thus provides a basis for inclusion of a faith-based approach to prisoner reentry" (p. 18). Sections include: the relevance of religion in prisons and prisoner reentry; faith-based prisoner reentry -- strengths and shortcomings; harnessing human and spiritual capital through intermediaries; a comprehensive and scalable prisoner reentry plan; and conclusion.

http://nicic.gov/Library/023276

Listwan, Shelley Johnson, Dena Hanley, and Mark Colvin. *The Prison Experience and Reentry: Examining the Impact of Victimization on Coming Home.* Washington, DC: National Institute of Justice, 2011.

The impact of prison victimization on how an offender behaves when released back into the community is examined. Sections following an abstract include: executive summary; introduction; review of the relevant literature; methodology; results for design and sample selection, prison victimization data, characteristics of selected victimization incidents, and re-entry outcomes; conclusion; and implications for policy and practice. A few of the observations made from the research are: about 58% of the sample experienced victimization; 97.9% witnessed someone being victimized; victims did take advantage of prison-based treatment; and younger offenders are more likely to be victims. "Ultimately, however, prison violence and subsequently re-entry outcomes, are likely to be impacted from a structured and deliberate response utilizing best practices in the areas of assessment and treatment" (p. 102).

http://nicic.gov/Library/026041

Parent, Dale G., and Cranston Mitchell. *Transition from Prison into Community: Project Briefing.* Cambridge, MA: Abt Associates, 2002.

Copies of overheads used in a presentation about the National Institute of Corrections' (NIC) Transition from Prison into Community project are supplied. Topics discussed include: transition reform -- the solution to adequately protecting the public while dealing with the record number of released prisoners; the NIC model -- a new transition process, reform promotion, partnership creation, and information sharing; key agencies in transition reform; phases of the initiative; involve the stakeholders; principles of the transition accountability plan (TAP); advantages of TAP; stakeholders involved in partnerships; transition partnerships; the need to share data; enhancing communication through technology; and transition performance measures.

http://nicic.gov/Library/020462

Pettway, Coretta. *Best Practices Tool-Kit: Faith/Based Programming, Reentry and Recidivism.* London, OH: Ohio Department of Rehabilitation and Correction, 2007.

Empirical evidence for the impact of religious activities and/or the effectiveness of faith-based programs is reviewed. Topics covered include: program implementation; highlighted program -- the InnerChange Freedom Initiative (IFI)); and legal concerns.

http://www.drc.state.oh.us/web/iej_files/FaithProgramming_Reentry_Reci divism.pdf

"Promising Strategies in Transition from Prison." *Topics in Community Corrections.* Annual Issue 2007. Longmont, CO: LIS, Inc., 2007.

Issue contents are: "Foreword" by Kermit Humphries; "An Overview of NIC's Transition from Prison to the Community Initiative" by Peggy B. Burke; "Rising to the Challenge of Applying Evidence-Based Practices Across the Spectrum of a State Parole Board" by Sherry Tate and Catherine C. McVey; "Collaboration and Partnership in the Community: Advancing the Michigan Prisoner ReEntry Initiative" by Le'Ann Duran; "Providing Tools for Risk Reduction Case Management in Parole and Community Corrections" by Keven Pellant and Margie Phelps; "Improving Parole Outcomes with Performance Leadership and Data: Doing What Works" by Danny Hunter, George Braucht, and John Prevost; "Working Together to Improve Reentry: Bridging Budgets and Programs, Public and Private, Prison and the Community" by Ginger Martin; "Ensuring Successful Offender Reentry: Umatilla/Morrow County "Reach-In" Services" by Mark Royal; "Creating Better Transitions at Indiana's Plainfield Reentry Educational Facility" by Michael Lloyd; "Gender-Responsive Reentry in Rhode Island: A Long and Winding Road" by Bree Derrick; and "Missouri Makes Its Move Toward a New Reentry Philosophy" by Julie Boehm.

http://nicic.gov/Library/022777

*State of Recidivism: The Revolving Door of America's Prisons.* Washington, DC: Pew Center on the States, 2011.

Anyone concerned with keeping ex-offenders out of prison or jail, be they correctional professionals or concerned community members, should read this publication. "This report seeks to elevate the public discussion about recidivism, prompting policy makers and the public to dig more deeply into the factors that impact rates of return to prison, and into effective strategies for reducing them" (p. 1). Sections following an executive summary are: introduction—recidivism as a performance measure, overview of the study, and what a recidivism rate is; a closer look at recidivism rates—new figures show steady national recidivism rate, states vary widely, and how recidivism rates have changed; unpacking the numbers—how sentencing impacts recidivism rate, how community corrections policy impacts recidivism rate, and examples of how three states dealt with recidivism; and improving public safety and cutting correctional costs—strategies for successfully reducing recidivism, resources for developing effective reentry and supervision strategies, and a promising start.

http://nicic.gov/Library/024981

Taxman, Faye S. "The Cattle Call of Reentry: Not all Processes are Equal." *Criminology & Public Policy,* 10: 925–937. http://onlinelibrary. wiley.com/doi/10.1111/j.1745-9133.2011.00780.x/abstract, 2011.

With budget crunches capturing the attention of state and local governments, the affordability of long prison (jail) sentences is being questioned. States have taken daring steps to use early release tactics, with the expectations that such moves will both save money and reduce recidivism. Kevin A. Wright and Jeffrey W. Rosky (2011, this issue) explored the impact of early release efforts in one state. Not surprisingly, the results are disappointing in that those individuals who were released early were more likely to recidivate than those who served their time. Wright and Rosky point to several explanations, including the potential actions of parole officers and other attributes covered under the umbrella of "criminal justice thermodynamics" where the mechanics of the criminal justice system continue working in such a fashion to "backfire." The findings of this study are predictable – early releases are more likely to recidivate – and those thrust back into society without preparation are doomed to fail. In this essay, I consider the importance of the messages that are attached to different policy initiatives, the messages that basically support the cattle call that "all things *should* work." Unless we focus on the messages and the "punitive culture," most of our efforts will fail to reform the justice system or people involved in justice environments. [abstract from author]

Taxman, Faye S., et al. *What Works in Residential Centers Monographs.* Fairfax, VA: George Mason University, 2010.

This series of monographs "examines the impact of participation in a RRC [Residential Re-entry Center] on federal offender release outcomes" (p. 2). RRCs assist in the transition of offenders from prison to the community. The series contains eight reports: Executive Overview: What Works in Residential Reentry Centers; Report 1: What Is the Impact of "Performance Contracting" on Offender Supervision Services?; Report 2: Measuring Performance- The Capacity of Residential Reentry Centers (RRCs) to Collect, Manage, and Analyze Client-Level Data; Report 3: What Organizational Factors Are Related to Improved Outcomes?; Report 4: How Do Staff Hiring, Retention, Management and Attitudes Affect Organizational Climate and Performance in RRCs?; Report 5: What Services Are Provided by RRCs?; Report 6: Technical Violation Rates and Rearrest Rates on Federal Probation after Release from an RRC; and Report 7: Site Visits. The rearrest rate for offenders who participated in RRCs is 13 % while technical violations that ended in revocation of supervised release is 23.5%.

http://nicic.gov/Library/025266

*Transition from Prison to Community: Making It Work [Satellite/Internet Broadcast]*. Longmont, CO: National Institute of Corrections Academy, 2005.

Public safety is everyone's business. This year, 600,000 offenders will leave prison and return to our communities. Whether released offenders live as law-abiding citizens or return to criminal behavior is largely dependent on the preparations made for their release while in prison and their transition process from prison to the community. Many jurisdictions have embraced NIC's Transition from Prison to Community (TPC) Model to increase public safety, support a successful transition process, and utilize scarce taxpayers dollars more effectively. The TPC Model involves community organizations and partnering agencies in creating system change that holds offenders accountable and supports their success in the community. This 3-hour program, originally broadcast September 28, 2005, focuses on the TPC implementation experiences of two states - Missouri and Michigan. Panelists will discuss their experiences with and insights to implementing the reentry model.

http://nicic.gov/Library/020490.

*Virginia Adult Re-entry Initiative: The Four Year Strategic Plan: Executive Summary: July 2010 - June 2014*. Richmond: Virginia Department of Corrections, 2011.

Those agencies needing to create a strategic plan for their own reentry programs will find common elements in this plan that they can use. Sections of this executive summary are: background; development of the Virginia Adult Re-entry Initiative (VARI) strategic plan; VARI strategic plan summary— vision, mission, principles, goals, service components (i.e., first contact, reception, on-going assessment and case planning, programs and services, re-entry service continuum from less than five years before release to lifers, the three phases of re-entry preparation, community supervision, and special populations; and concluding comments. Related flow charts also provided include: the Virginia re-entry structure; Transition from Prison to the Community (TPC) model; Virginia adult re-entry program model; programs and re-entry; and correctional control and offender personal responsibility.

http://www.vadoc.virginia.gov/documents/reentryInitiativeExecSummary. pdf

## REENTRY – COMMUNITY AND FAMILY SUPPORT

Bilchik, Shay, *et al. Family Engagement in Reentry for Justice-Involved Youth.* New York: National Reentry Resource Center, 2010.

Four presentations regarding the need for families to be involved in the reentry process for released youth are contained in this document. The presentations include: the Family Justice Program—defining family broadly, strength-based approach, impact of family and other social support on reentry outcomes, youth voices, juvenile corrections staff survey, probation and correctional leaders survey, and youth genograms; a family-focused approach to juvenile corrections—California Department of Correction and Rehabilitation Division of Juvenile Justice; engaging families in the community—Adolescent Portable Therapy (APT); and a movement of change—national examples of integrating a family-focused, strength-based approach.

http://www.nationalreentryresourcecenter.org/documents/0000/0775/Oct_4_Webinar_Slides_FINAL.pdf

Brazzell, Diana, *et al. From the Classroom to the Community: Exploring the Role of Education during Incarceration and Reentry.* New York: City University of New York, John Jay College of Criminal Justice, Prison Reentry Institute, 2009.

This monograph examines the "current state of education during education and reentry and identifie[s] promising programmatic and policy directions" (p. 3). Parts contained in this publication include: introduction—education, reincarceration, and reentry; the current landscape of education during incarceration and reentry; research on the effectiveness of correctional education; education behind the walls—challenges and opportunities; from classroom to community—education and reentry.

http://nicic.gov/Library/024041

Christian, Johnna, *et al. Bringing Families In: Recommendations of the Incarceration, Reentry and the Family Roundtables.* Newark: New Jersey Institute for Social Justice, Rutgers University, 2006.

Recommendations for "facilitating the connections between [New Jersey] prisoners and their families and in preparing both for the process of reentry" are given (p. 3). Central findings and recommendations are provided for Department of Correction (DOC), State Parole Board, Department of Human Services (DHS) and the Department of Children and Families, Juvenile Justice

Commission (JJC), family members, incarcerated individuals, community based organizations, advocacy groups, universities/educational institutions, and Department of Education/schools.

http://www.njisj.org/document/FinalRecommendations.pdf

*Community-Supervision: Using a Strength-Based, Family-Focused Approach* [Satellite/Internet Broadcast]. Longmont, CO. National Institute of Corrections Academy, 2005.

This 3-hour program, originally broadcast March 16, 2005, will help professionals identify the strengths and resources inherent in the family as a fundamental support system for individuals upon their release from prison or jail. It is designed to stimulate new ways of thinking about the family as a resource to enhance offender reentry and supervision and to increase public safety. The goal of this broadcast is to encourage participants to think about: enhancing the reentry and supervision processes through contextual thinking about the family; tapping the strengths of families and communities as means of good government to enhance public safety; utilizing family and community resources after government intervention has ended; and addressing the challenge of negotiating multiple services that may be used by the family to enhance positive outcomes.

*The Connections Project*. Germantown, MD: National Fatherhood Initiative, 2011.

If your agency is looking for ways to reduce the recidivism of fathers returning to the community, this program might be for you. "The Connections Project is an initiative that focuses on the power of engaged fathers for successful reentry." This website provides access to information about Connections, tools for practitioners, tools for fathers, the Connections Forum, success stories, and contact information.

http://www.fatherhood.org/theconnectionsproject/

Crayton, Anna, *et al. Partnering with Jails to Improve Reentry: A Guidebook for Community-Based Organizations*. Washington DC: Urban Institute, 2010.

Anyone looking to create a partnership between a community-based organization (CBO) and a jail reentry program will find this publication very helpful. This guidebook is divided into these sections: introduction; understanding the big picture, incarceration and jail reentry; developing and sustaining a partnership with the local jail; working with the jail population and in the jail environment; examples of strong partnerships between CBOs and jails; resources for the field; and conclusion. Appendixes provide sample memoranda of understanding, sample release of information forms, and partnership profiles.

http://nicic.gov/Library/024702

*Engaging Fathers for Successful Reentry: Research, Tips, Best Practices.* Germantown, MD: National Fatherhood Initiative, 2011.

A selection of fact sheets "connect the dots between eight of the most significant reentry challenges and the need to engage incarcerated and reentering fathers in becoming better dads" (p. 3). This report covers housing, employment, marriage and relationships, substance abuse, mentoring and community support, child support, involving moms, and domestic violence.

http://nicic.gov/Library/025155

Hairston, Creasie Finney, *et al. Coming Home from Prison: Family Matters.* London, OH: Institute for Excellence in Justice, 2008.

Access to keynote remarks, comments, Q and A, presentations, and handouts from a seminar on the impact of families on community reentry are available at this website. "Families as sources of support, conflict and domestic violence, parent-child relationships, and parole practices and expectations are among the topics covered" (p. 1).

http://nicic.gov/Library/023182

Leverentz, Andrea M. *People, Places, and Things: The Social Process of Reentry for Female Ex-Offenders.* Washington, DC: National Institute of Justice, 2006.

The process of and factors that impact the reentry of female ex-offenders are investigated. Chapters following an abstract are: issues in female offending and reentry; methodology; origins of offending; intimate relationships and desistance -- family; romantic relationships and friends; education and employment; housing and neighborhood; and the social context of reentry.

http://www.ncjrs.gov/pdffiles1/nij/grants/215178.pdf

Nellis, Ashley, Richard Hooks Wayman, and Sara Schirmer. *Back on Track: Supporting Youth Reentry from Out-of-Home Placement to the Community.* Washington, DC: U.S. Department of Justice, Office of Juvenile Justice and Delinquency Prevention, 2009.

"Public safety is compromised when youth leaving out-of-home placements are not afforded necessary supportive services upon reentering their communities and are therefore at great risk to recidivate into criminal behavior" (p.5). This report provides guidance and recommendations for achieving successful reentry services and programs. Sections following an executive summary are: introduction; characteristics of reentry youth; collateral consequences associated with out-of-home placement; essential components of youth reentry services; effective outcomes for youth reentry; federal support for reentry in the child welfare system; principles for effective youth reentry; and recommendations for federal leadership in youth reentry.

http://nicic.gov/Library/024165

Pettway, Coretta. *Best Practices Tool-Kit: Family Involvement during Incarceration and Reentry.* London, OH: Ohio Department of Rehabilitation and Correction, 2008.

Aims to identify empirical evidence regarding strategies, programs and practices geared toward family involvement during incarceration and reentry. Topics include family of the incarcerated, families and reentry, maintaining and facilitating familial involvement, and exemplary programs.

http://nicic.gov/Library/023181

*Ready4Reentry Prisoner Reentry Toolkit for Faith-Based and Community Organizations.* Washington, DC: Center for Faith-Based and Community Initiatives, 2008.

A promising practices guide for small to medium sized faith-based and community organizations interested in starting or bolstering reentry efforts. Nine sections are contained in this publication: launching a reentry organization; designing an effective program structure; forming successful partnerships; recruiting clients and volunteers; crafting intensive case management; removing barriers to employment through supportive services; implementing effectual employment preparation; succeeding at job placement; mentoring adult ex-prisoners; monitoring program success; and conclusion.

http://www.doleta.gov/PRI/PDF/Pritoolkit.pdf

Shanahan, Ryan, and Sandra Villalobos Agudelo. *Close to Home: Building on Family Support for People Leaving Jail.* New York: Vera Institute of Justice, Family Justice Program, 2011. Most research and programming about incarcerated people and their family support systems focus on prison settings. Because jail is substantially different from prison—most notably, time served there is usually shorter—it is not clear that policies and practices that work in prisons can be applied successfully in jails. This report describes the Family Justice Program's Close to Home project, which implemented the Relational Inquiry Tool (RIT)—a series of questions originally designed for and tested in prisons to stimulate incarcerated people's thinking about supportive family members as a resource—in three jails in Maryland and Wisconsin. The report also discusses the results from qualitative and quantitative research at the three facilities, aimed at gauging the attitudes of jail staff, incarcerated men and women, and family members toward the RIT.

http://www.vera.org/content/close-home-building-family-support-people-leaving-jail

Solomon, Amy L., *et al. Prisoner Reentry: Addressing the Challenges in Weed and Seed Communities.* Washington, DC: Urban Institute, Justice Policy Center, 2006.

The ways in which Weed and Seed sites provide offender reentry programs and partner with local organizations is surveyed. Sections of this report cover: Weed and Seed involvement in prisoner reentry; target populations for reentry programs; reentry programs and strategies; program size; expected outcomes; partner organizations in Weed and Seed reentry efforts; the Weed and Seed/VISTA (Volunteers in Service to America) Reentry Initiative; innovative practices involving housing, employment, family, and community; barriers to reentry programming; technical assistance needs; experienced Weed and Seed sites are a resource; and looking forward.

http://www.urban.org/UploadedPDF/411364_prisoner_reentry.pdf

*Straight-Up: (Expanding) Mentoring of Current and Formerly Incarcerated Adults: Key Components of Successful Relationship-Building to Support Positive Change.* Blaine, WA: National Coalition of Community-Based Correctional and Community Re-Entry Service Organizations, 2011.

"This paper contributes to identifying the determinants and characteristics of successful mentoring in the corrections and re-entry context. This analysis has application for formal mentors as well as for other front-line correctional staff and volunteers who seek effective interaction skills when engaging with current and formerly incarcerated individuals" (p. 3). Findings cover: mentoring as a support for positive post-prison outcomes; the context for mentoring relationships within corrections and reentry; the role of the mentorship-style of leadership; what mentoring is; the degree to which mentoring is effective; who is most likely to benefit from mentoring;

identifying and selecting individuals for mentor guidance; demographics and mentoring; the relationships between a mentor and offender; and how to mentor.

http://www.nc4rso.org/Straight%20Up%20Mentoring%20of%20Current %20and%20Formerly%20Incarcerated%20Individuals.pdf

*They're Coming Back: An Action Plan for Successful Reintegration of Offenders that Works for Everyone.* Philadelphia, PA: Philadelphia Consensus Group on Reentry and Reintegration of Adjudicated Offenders, 2002.

Strategies for implementing effective reintegration programs and interventions are provided. Following an executive summary, findings and recommendations are organized into five topic areas: personal empowerment, responsibility, and reconciliation; pre-release; legal; employment, education, and training; and community integration.

http://www.fcnetwork.org/reading/philadelphiareentry.pdf

Travis, Jeremy, and Michelle Waul, eds. *Prisoners Once Removed: The Impact of Incarceration and Reentry on Children, Families, and Communities.* Washington, DC: Urban Institute Press, 2003.

The impact of incarceration upon the prisoners themselves, the relationships between parents and children, and service networks is explored. Chapters in this book include: "Prisoners Once Removed: The Children and Families of Prisoners" by Jeremy Travis and Michelle Waul; "The Psychological Impact of Incarceration: Implications for Postprison Adjustment" by Craig Haney; "A Woman's Journey Home: Challenges for Female Offenders" by Stephanie S. Covington; "The Skill Sets and Health Care Needs of Released Offenders" by Gerald G. Gaes and Newton Kendig; "From One Generation to the Next: How Criminal Sanctions Are Reshaping Family Life in Urban America" by Donald Braman and Jenifer Wood; "The Effects of Parental Incarceration on Children: Perspectives, Promises, and Policies" by Ross D. Parke and K. Alison Clarke-Stewart; "The Adolescent Children of Incarcerated Parents: A Developmental Perspective" by J. Mark Eddy and John B. Reid; "Prisoners and Their Families: Parenting Issues During Incarceration" by Creasie Finney Hairston; "Criminal Justice and Health and Human Services: An Exploration of Overlapping Needs, Resources, and Interests in Brooklyn Neighborhoods" by Eric Cadora, Charles wartz, and Mannix Gordon; "Incarceration, Reentry, and Social Capital: Social Networks in the Balance" by Dina R. Rose and Todd R. Clear; and "Building

Partnerships to Strengthen Offenders, Families, and Communities" by Shelli Balter Rossman.

VanDeCarr, Paul. *Call to Action: How Programs in Three Cities Responded to the Prisoner Reentry Crisis.* Philadelphia, PA: Public/Private Ventures, 2007.

"This report is the story of how programs in three cities responded to the reentry crisis, before they became part of the Ready4Work initiative" (p. 2). Chapters comprising this publication include: introduction -- getting out; Jacksonville (FL) case study -- a journey in progress; Memphis (TN) case study -- hearing the call; Washington, DC case study -- the most positive thing; and conclusion -- pioneers in reentry. Elements of a successful reentry program, be they internal components or external relations, are described.

http://www.ppv.org/ppv/publications/assets/211_publication.pdf

Visher, Christy, Tobi Palmer, and Caterina Gouvis Roman. *Cleveland Stakeholders' Perceptions of Prisoner Reentry.* Washington, DC: Urban Institute, Justice Policy Center, 2007.

"This policy brief presents findings from interviews with stakeholders -- specific persons or organizations -- familiar with issues affecting individuals transitioning from prison to the community" (p. 1). Topics discussed include: barriers affecting successful reentry -- housing, employment, social services, community perception and public stigma, and personal barriers; solutions and suggested changes to policy and practice; the role of government agencies in addressing reentry; prison reentry in Ohio - an overview; finding from interviews with former prisoners; and City of Cleveland's reentry strategy.

http://www.urban.org/UploadedPDF/411515_cleveland_prisoner_reentry.pdf

Yoon, Jamie, and Jessica Nickel. *Reentry Partnerships: A Guide for States & Faith-Based and Community Organizations.* Washington, DC: U.S. Bureau of Justice Assistance, 2008.

Recommendations are given on how states "can improve reentry, reduce recidivism, and build or improve collaborations with community-based service providers" (p. 3). Goals and recommendations explain how to: build and sustain comprehensive networks with faith-based and community organizations; simplify pathways to funding for reentry initiatives; tailor responses to the population that will be served by a reentry initiative; and how to ensure accountability for efficient use of funds and gather critical data.

http://nicic.gov/Library/023485


# REENTRY – EMPLOYMENT AND HOUSING

Bishop, Catherine. *An Affordable Home on Re-Entry: Federally Assisted Housing and Previously Incarcerated Individuals.* Oakland, CA: National Housing Law Project, 2008.

"This guide is designed for advocates working with or representing individuals with a criminal record who are seeking access to federally assisted housing programs" (p. 1). Chapters include: the problem -- the number of individuals who have been incarcerated is increasing and many need affordable housing; eligibility for federally assisted housing for individuals who have been released from incarceration; access to criminal history records, drug rehabilitation information, and expungement of criminal records; mitigating circumstances and rehabilitation; challenging a denial of admission; advocating for policies that respond to the housing needs of individuals with a criminal record; vouchers, portability, and ex-offenders; adding an ex-offender to the assisted household and rechecking current residents; description of federally assisted housing programs for lower income families; and general eligibility requirements for federally assisted low-income housing.

http://nicic.gov/Library/023734


*Building Tomorrow's Workforce: An Effective Reentry Strategy [Satellite/Internet Broadcast].* Aurora, CO: National Institute of Corrections Academy, 2008.

This 3-hour program, originally broadcast August 2008, focused on the history and benefits of correctional industries and ways to balance competing interests. Employment is a critical factor in successful reentry. Career assistance, life skills, and job training prior to release from jails or prisons increases the likelihood of success as individuals reenter the community. This, in conjunction with support from employers, social agencies, and faith-based community organizations, provides the foundation for individuals to remain in society and contribute to the community as productive citizens. At the end of this broadcast, participants will understand the: benefits of correctional industries and workforce development; social and economic values of correctional industries; need to strike a balance between competing interests; relationships among workforce development, community organizations, and correctional industries; relationship between evidence-based practices and offender employment; and workforce development competencies and available training resources.

http://nicic.gov/Library/023255

Carter, Francina. *Get the Facts: Dispelling the Myths about Ex-Offenders.* Washington DC: National Association of Workforce Development Professionals, 2012.

"Regardless of your workplace setting, you will probably encounter someone with a criminal record. Workforce development professionals need the facts about strategies and services that help to reduce the barriers to employment and support services faced by their clients with criminal records … [One] will learn: 1. What the federal policy actually restricts; 2. Where to find resources and fact sheets that will help explain the rights of ex-offenders; 3. Strategies for working with local officials to address unnecessary barriers that inhibit individuals from gaining employment; [and] 4. Ideas for framing the conversation with employers."

http://www.nawdp.org/Content/NavigationMenu/WorkforceDevelopment/eLearning/Dispelling_the_Myths.htm

*Correctional Industries: A Working Solution [Satellite/Internet Broadcast].* Washington, DC: National Institute of Corrections, 2011.

Correctional Industry programs contribute to the successful reentry of offenders by providing a structured environment for participants to learn the skills needed to obtain and retain post-release employment. Guided by evidence-based practices, Correctional Industries distinguishes itself by providing services that make an impact in reducing inmate recidivism. See how they make a significant difference in the lives of the offender population they serve and hear from national experts, correctional practitioners, and former offenders about the promising and evidenced-practices that impact recidivism. At the conclusion of this program broadcast on October 5, 2011, participants will be able to: describe the evolution of Correctional Industries from "producing quality products" to "developing individuals who produce quality products"; explain how the incorporation of evidence-based practices helps improve program outcomes; identify how Correctional Industries provides offenders with the skills they need to successfully obtain and retain post-release employment; and identify evidence-based training opportunities that promote professional growth and development.

http://nicic.gov/Library/025293

Cortes, Katherine, and Shawn Rogers. *Reentry Housing Options: The Policymakers' Guide*. New York: Council of State Governments Justice Center, 2010.

This guide is for those people wanting to reduce the recidivism of offenders returning to the community by offering plenty of affordable housing. Sections of this report include: introduction; the unmet demand for affordable housing; reentry housing options charts; three approaches to increasing housing capacity for the reentry population; housing terms; laying the groundwork for increasing reentry housing capacity; greater access; increased housing stock; revitalized neighborhoods; and conclusion.

http://nicic.gov/Library/024426

Emsellem, Maurice, and Madeline Neighly. *Cities Pave the Way: Promising Reentry Policies that Promote Local Hiring of People with Criminal Records*. Washington, DC: National League of Cities Institute for Youth, Education and Families, 2010.

Individuals involved with helping ex-offenders find employment after their release from incarceration will find this guide very interesting. It "assembles the most promising local policies that promote the hiring of people with criminal records" (p.1). Seven parts are contained in this publication: introduction; the basics, the city hiring process; three steps to a model city hiring policy; leverage development funds to target jobs for people with criminal records; expanding bid incentive programs to promote local hiring priorities; financial incentives for private employers to create jobs for people with criminal records; and conclusion.

http://nicic.gov/Library/024622

*Enhancing Rural Reentry through Housing Partnerships: A Handbook for Community Corrections Agencies in Rural Areas*. New York: Family Justice, 2009.

This handbook "discuss[es] potentially beneficial partnerships that community corrections departments can cultivate to fully tap resources and expertise . . . [and] also suggests various strategies to increase housing options for people coming home from jail and prison -- and for their families" (p. 5). Sections contained in this document include: introduction; defining rural; high-need rural areas; affordable housing challenges in rural areas; rural homelessness; rural reentry issues; housing and reentry -- an overview; strategies for engaging families; potential strategies for community corrections; the role of corrections agencies; case studies; and relevant laws and policies.

http://nicic.gov/Library/023976

*An Evaluation of the Prisoner Reentry Initiative: Final Report.* St. Paul: Minnesota Department of Corrections, 2011.

The impact of Minnesota's Prisoner Reentry Initiative (PRI) on post-release employment and recidivism are evaluated. Two case assistant/reentry coordinators were place within the criminal justice system, not outside it, in order to better facilitate interagency connections between facility and community-based staff. This report is necessary reading for agencies thinking of implementing a similar offender employment system. Sections of this report include an executive summary, a description of PRI, data and methods, results, and conclusion. While recidivism rates for PRI participants were not much lower than the comparison group, PRI "participation significantly reduced the chances of finding post-release employment and that participants worked significantly fewer hours and had significantly less total earnings" (p. 5).

http://nicic.gov/Library/025634

*First Policy Paper Series on Issues Affecting the Employment of Former Offenders in Illinois: Four Papers.* Chicago, IL: Safer Foundation, 2002.

Four policy papers examining the systemic barriers to ex-offender employment are presented. Papers include: "The Need for Public Policy Advocacy to Reduce Barriers to Employment for Ex-Offenders" by Sharron D. Matthews; "Reducing Barriers to Employment for Women Ex-Offenders: Mapping the Road to Reintegration" by Patricia O'Brien; "Government Personnel Policies Impacting the Hiring of Ex-Offenders" by Matthews and Amanda Casarjian; and "A Review of the State of Illinois Professional and Occupational Licensure Policies as Related to Access to Employment for Ex-Offenders" by Matthews, Ray Auclaire, and Amanda Casarjian.

http://web.archive.org/web/20061005054212/http://www.saferfoundation.org/viewpage.asp?id=312

Fontaine, Jocelyn, and Jennifer Biess. *Housing as a Platform for Formerly Incarcerated Persons.* Washington, DC: Urban Institute, 2012.

People who deal with offender reentry should read this. "Against the backdrop of the reentry challenges, this paper discusses how housing can be a platform or pathway toward more successful reentry and reintegration for formerly incarcerated persons. While housing for formerly incarcerated persons is a source of necessary shelter and residential stability, it can also serve as the literal and figurative foundation for successful reentry and reintegration for released adults" (p. 1). Sections of this publication include: introduction; overview of reentry challenges; housing as a complex reentry challenge; housing options and barriers; housing as a platform of formerly incarcerated individuals; the pathways model; potential plan for future analysis; and conclusion.

http://www.urban.org/publications/412552.html

Goldfarb and Lipman. *Between the Lines: A Question & Answer Guide on Legal Issues in Supportive Housing: 2010 National Edition.* Oakland, CA: Corporation for Supportive Housing, 2010.

Individuals assisting ex-offenders in finding housing should be familiar with this publication. Chapters include: why read this guide; legal overview—how the law is organized and fair housing laws; serving designated populations—introduction, reserving housing for people with disabilities, economic discrimination, projects serving homeless people, and discrimination based on source of income, and restricting housing to other groups; selection of individual tenants—screening and intake and reasonable accommodations and reasonable modifications; operation and management of housing--accommodation and modification during occupancy, providing services to tenants, clean and sober requirements, and other management issues; and zoning and land use. Appendixes provide a look at federal and state fair housing laws.

http://nicic.gov/Library/024516

*In Our Backyard: Overcoming Community Resistance To Reentry Housing (A NIMBY Toolkit).* Long Island City, NY: Fortune Society, 2011.

The development of a housing project in West Harlem for formerly incarcerated people is described. Organizations trying to find ways to house recently released inmates in the community should read this publication. Sections of this toolkit in addition to a summary include: the reentry crisis; a case study of the Fortune Academy project; what the Fortune Academy story tells us; and best practices for gaining community support—applying lessons learned to your organization.

http://nicic.gov/Library/025305

*Innovative Reentry Strategies: The Emerging Role of Correctional Industries [Satellite/Internet Broadcast].* Washington, DC: National Institute of Corrections, 2009.

This 3-hour program, originally broadcast October 7, 2009, is part 2 of the National Institute of Corrections series on correctional industries and is entitled "Innovative Reentry Strategies: The Emerging Role of Correctional Industries." Part 1, which aired in August 2008, focused on the history and benefits of correctional industries and ways to balance competing interests. The October 2009 program will focus on presenting new reentry strategies and highlight specific programs around the country that reflect best practices. Imagine a reentry program that reduces recidivism, changes lives, and makes prisons and jails safer with little or no cost to taxpayers. Such a program has been around for decades. It is correctional industries, an effective model for preparing offenders for employment upon release. The elements of this strategy include skills certification, positive change, collaboration with businesses and the community, and a focus on career development and job retention.

http://nicic.gov/Library/024019

mms://tpt.wmod.llnwd.net/a3757/o33/20091007_NIC_DV_CC.wmv

Latessa, Edward. "Why Work is Important, and How to Improve the Effectiveness of Correctional Reentry Programs that Target Employment." *Criminology & Public Policy* 11, no. 1. (2012): 87-91.

Latessa discusses the importance of employment and the effectiveness of correctional reentry programs that target employment. First, work and employment is important for reentry and they should not ignore it simply because most studies have not shown employment programs to reduce recidivism. Second, the nature of risk factors is more complex than simply categorizing them into static and dynamic. There are different types of dynamic factors, and they can see this clearly when looking at employment. Third, if they truly want to incorporate employment into effective correctional programs, they need to employ techniques and approaches that have been found to be effective in changing behavior.

http://onlinelibrary.wiley.com/doi/10.1111/j.1745-9133.2012.00790.x/abstract

MacDonald, Stephen, and Carl Nink. *Industry Recognized Certification: A Pathway to Reentry.* Centerville UT: MTC Institute, 2011.

The use of industry-based certification to increase the likelihood that ex-offenders will succeed in finding jobs is explained. Certification plays a vital role because the "reentry success of inmates requires that they develop skills consistent with industry standards and that they obtain recognized and marketable certification, which employers often use as one important criterion for hiring" (p. 1). Sections compiling this publication are: introduction; need for skilled labor; need for certification; certifications for corrections; available certifications; possible certifications; conclusion; certifying organizations; employment opportunities and median wage; what a Career Readiness Certificate (CRC) is; and Internet use in prisons (limited, secure, and virtual).

http://www.mtctrains.com/public/uploads/1/2011/7/A%20Pathway%20to %20Reentry.

*Offender Employment Retention: Worth the Work [Satellite/Internet Broadcast]*. Aurora, CO: National Institute of Corrections Academy, 2011. According to the Bureau of Justice Statistics, more than 700,000 individuals are released from prisons yearly—with an additional 9 million adults cycling through local jails. Research indicates that employment is an important component of successful reentry, but most offender programs do not address the complex behavioral health issues that impact the offender's ability to obtain and retain gainful employment while remaining crime free. Offender programming should target individuals at high risk for recidivism, address the dynamic influences that predict crime, and provide interventions specific to the needs of offenders. During this national discussion sponsored and broadcast by the National Institute of Corrections on November 2, 2011, participants will explore evidence-based practices that increase public safety while helping to reduce recidivism. At the conclusion of this broadcast, participants will be able to: define and describe an offender retention model; identify strategies, resources, and partnerships that improve retention outcomes; describe a process for developing effective offender services/programming; and identify collaborative partnerships that support increased public safety and effective reentry programs.

http://nicic.gov/Library/024978
http://tpt.wmod.llnwd.net/a3757/o33/NIC_11_02_2011.wmv

Pettway, Coretta. *Best Practices Tool-Kit: Employing Ex-Offenders after Release from Prison*. London, OH: Ohio Department of Rehabilitation and Correction, 2007.

Promising practices for adult offender job training and retention programming are described. Topics discussed include: implementing programs and services; and exemplary programs -- Safer Foundation, Ready4Work, Center for Employment Opportunities' Comprehensive Prison Reentry Program, and Project Re-Integration of Ex-Offenders (RIO).

http://www.drc.state.oh.us/web/iej_files/Employing_Ex-Offenders.pdf

*Women and Work: Gender Responsivity and Workforce Development [Satellite/Internet Broadcast].* Aurora, CO: National Institute of Corrections Academy, 2008.

This 2-day training program, originally broadcast September 24-25, 2008, will enable participants to: introduce emerging evidence-based gender responsive practices; present information strategies and case management models; introduce career theories and assessment tools; discuss collaborative relationships that support effective reentry; provide answers for the questions asked by women returning to the workforce; discuss how a history of criminal convictions impacts job search efforts; and discuss and present available resources and training options.

http://nicic.gov/Library/023548

Yahner, Jennifer, and Janine M. Zweig. *Which Components of Transitional Jobs Programs Work Best? Analysis of Programs for Former Prisoners in the Transitional Jobs Reentry Demonstration.* Washington, DC: Urban Institute, 2012

An evaluation of the Transitional Jobs Reentry Demonstration (TJRD) was implemented in order to discover which components of the TJRD positively impact outcomes. Results are provided for TJ (transitional job) program components associated with employment outcomes and with recidivism outcomes, which seemed to work best, whether effects vary across offender subgroups, and how many days in a TJ are best. "Overall, we observed a pattern of findings indicating that one TJ program component in particular was significantly associated with higher levels of subsequent unsubsidized employment among TJ program participants. That component measured the length of time that participants spent working in a transitional job" (p. 12).

http://www.urban.org/publications/412571.html

## REENTRY – HEALTH AND SAFETY

*Advocacy Toolkits to Combat Legal Barriers Facing Individuals with Criminal Records*. New York: Legal Action Center, 2011
Strategies for reducing the challenges faced by ex-offenders reentering their communities are explained by this series of Toolkits. Each kit contains sections regarding what the roadblock is, problems associated with it, and ways to change it, what advocates can do, model laws, Action Alerts, sample advocacy letters, (soon to be included) sample editorials for media outreach. Available Toolkits are: Prohibit Inquiries About Arrests That Never Led to Conviction; Standards for Hiring People with Criminal Records; Certificates of Rehabilitation; Sealing/Expunging Arrest and Conviction Records; Limiting Suspension/Revocation of Drivers' Licenses to Driving-Related Convictions; Improving Housing Opportunities for Individuals with Conviction Records; Opting Out of the Federal Ban on Food Stamps and Temporary Assistance to Needy Families (TANF); Working to Ensure that Individuals Who Can Safely Parent Have an Opportunity To Be Prospective Foster and Adoptive Parents; Restoring Medicaid Upon Release from Prison; Securing Official Identification for Individuals Leaving Prisons and Jails Valid State Identification Cards; Primary Funding Streams Available to Assist People with Criminal Records; Enforce Anti-Discrimination Laws; and How to Use Byrne Justice Assistance Grants.
http://nicic.gov/Library/025514

Bobbitt, Mike, Robin Campbell, and Gloria L. Tate. *Safe Return: Working Toward Preventing Domestic Violence When Men Return from Prison*. New York: Vera Institute of Justice, 2006.
Observations from a roundtable on the prevention of intimate partner violence perpetrated by individuals recently released from prison are reported. This publication covers: what is known about domestic violence and prisoner reentry; domestic violence among African Americans experiencing poverty; convening the roundtable discussions; selecting roundtable participants; key themes -- institutional resistance to dealing with domestic violence and reentry, when and how to add domestic violence work to current reentry efforts, supporting women and their children in the reentry process, building cultural competence and dealing with distrust of authorities, and integrating coordinated community responses into reentry plans; sheriff's anti-violence effort; African American program; what cultural competence is; roundtable participants -- where their practices are now; and summary and conclusion.

http://www.vera.org/download?file=3031/SRIRoundtable_Final.pdf

*Building an Offender Reentry Program: A Guide for Law Enforcement.*
Alexandria, VA: International Association of Chiefs of Police, 2006.
Information about the development and implementation of offender
reentry initiatives by law enforcement agencies is provided. Sections
comprising this guide are: offender reentry 101; building an offender reentry
program; current state of practice examples from law enforcement; glossary;
and additional sources.
http://www.theiacp.org/LinkClick.aspx?fileticket=ocK1XtwlyIA%3d&tab
id=253

Davis, Lois M., *et al. Understanding the Public Health Implications of
Prisoner Reentry in California: State-of-the-State Report.* Santa Monica, CA:
RAND Infrastructure, safety, and Environment, 2011.
"In particular, RAND examines the public health issues surrounding
prisoner reentry in California, the type of health care needs ex-offenders bring
with them, which communities are disproportionately affected, and the health
care system capacity of the communities to which ex-offenders return. The
research team also examined in depth the experiences of returning prisoners in
seeking care and the role that health plays in their efforts to reintegrate into the
community and rejoin their families; and factors that have facilitated or
hindered ex- prisoners' ability to obtain health care and providers' efforts to
serve them. In addition, the research team sought to explore the impact that
incarceration has on families, including what challenges they face and the need
for programs and services" (p. iii-iv). Six chapters are contained in this report:
introduction; what we know about prisoners' health care needs and the
capacity of the safety net to meet the needs of the reentry population;
understanding the challenges of reentry—ex-prisoner focus group results;
understanding the challenges of dealing with released prisoners—provider
interview results; the impact of incarceration on children and families; and
conclusions and recommendations.
http://nicic.gov/Library/026397

*Establishing and Maintaining Medicaid Eligibility upon Release from
Public Institutions.* Rockville, MD: Substance Abuse and Mental Health
Services Administration, 2010.
Individuals involved in acquiring Medicaid benefits for mentally ill ex-
offenders returning to the community will find the lessons learned from this

study helpful. The development and implementation of "a model program to ensure that eligible individuals with mental illness were enrolled in Medicaid at discharge from state institutions" was evaluated (p.1). Five sections follow an executive summary: introduction; barriers to ensuring Medicaid eligibility for adults leaving state institutions; increasing Medicaid coverage on release for correctional facilities, results of a model program in Oklahoma; Medicaid eligibility of clients in an institution for mental diseases, a case study from Oklahoma; and synthesis of study findings—lessons learned about program implementation, quantitative results, and potential for implementing similar programs.

http://store.samhsa.gov/shin/content/SMA10-4545/SMA10-4545.pdf
http://nicic.gov/Library/024645


*Facilitating Medicaid Enrollment for People with Serious Mental Illnesses Leaving Jail or Prison: Key Questions for Policymakers Committed to Improving Health and Policy Safety.* New York: Council of State Governments, 2011.

The access to Medicaid and Supplemental Security Income/Social Security Disability Insurance (SSI/SSDI) that justice-involved people with serious mental illness (SMI) should have is an area of frequent confusion. Answers to questions which "can help policymakers facilitate or strengthen effective collaboration among corrections, health, and mental health agencies to identify and enroll eligible individuals with SMI in these programs" are provided (p. 1). Reasons for why policymakers should care about and ways to determine answers to the following are explained: what is the percentage of the total corrections population is eligible for Medicaid and of these how many have SMI and of those how many are eligible for SSI/SSDI; how a corrections system identifies individuals at intake who meet the new Medicaid income guidelines and who also have SMI; and at what point prior to an individual's release the corrections system begins the application process for Medicaid and SSI/SSDI.

http://nicic.gov/Library/025574


Jannetta, Jesse, and Pamela Lachman. *Promoting Partnerships between Police and Community Supervision Agencies: How Coordination Can Reduce Crime and Improve Public Safety.* Washington, DC: U.S. Dept. of Justice, Community Oriented Policing Services (COPS), 2011.

The key role a partnership between local law enforcement and community supervision agencies plays in offender reentry is explained. Individuals seeking to reduce recidivism and ensure public safety should read this guide. Sections of this publication include: partnership benefits; partnership contributions; key partnership elements—intelligence and information sharing, case planning and supporting behavior change, problem-solving approaches, emphasis on special populations, and focused deterrence; challenges for supervision/police partnerships; and conclusion. Appendixes provide sample Welcome Home Letter, Search and Seizure Legislation, and Liaison Office Job Description. There are also nine partnership examples spread throughout the text.

    http://www.urban.org/uploadedpdf/412362-promoting-partnerships-police-community-supervision-agencies.pdf

*Keys to Federal Benefits Access.* New York: Reentry Policy Council, 2011.

Identifies key issue areas for policymakers seeking to ensure that people who are eligible for SSI/SSDI and Medicaid are enrolled immediately upon release.

    http://nicic.gov/Library/025572

La Vigne, Nancy G., *et al. Prisoner Reentry and Community Policing: Strategies for Enhancing Public Safety.* Washington, DC: Urban Institute/ Justice Policy Center, 2006.

The relationship between prisoner reentry and community policing while ensuring public safety is investigated. This report is divided into the following parts: introduction; what the impact of prisoner reentry is on public safety; why police should have a role in prisoner reentry; examples from the field; challenges for police reentry partnerships; and looking forward.

    http://www.urban.org/UploadedPDF/411061_COPS_reentry_monograph.pdf

Mallik-Kane, Kamala, and Christy A. Visher. *Health and Prisoner Reentry: How Physical, Mental, and Substance Abuse Conditions Shape the Process of Reintegration.* Washington, DC: Urban Institute/Justice Policy Center, 2008.

The degree to which physical health, mental illness, and substance abuse impact prisoners' reentry is examined. Six chapters follow an executive summary: introduction; prisoner reentry -- an overview; physical health and reentry; mental health and reentry; substance abuse and reentry; and discussion and policy implications. Most of the returning prisoners have chronic health problems -- 90% female and 80% men. The likelihood of reincarceration is higher for those returning prisoners having bad health, be it physical, mental, or substance abuse.

http://nicic.gov/Library/022922

*Offender Re-Entry: Exploring the Leadership Opportunity for Law Enforcement Executives and Their Agencies: Final Report of the IACP/COPS 2006 Summit.* Alexandria, VA: International Association of Chiefs of Police, 2007.

Recommendations are provided that will guide law enforcement executives and their agencies in their work to transition offenders from prison to productive life while protecting the public from those who will re-offend. Fifty recommendations follow an executive summary and are organized according to these areas: asserting leadership; identifying funding; collaborating with community stakeholders; designing offender re-entry efforts; training agencies and community partners; educating the public; and cultivating public support.

http://www.theiacp.org/PublicationsGuides/TopicalIndex/tabid/216/Default.aspx?id=1109&v=1

Schwarzfeld, Matt, *et al. Planning and Assessing a Law Enforcement Reentry Strategy.* New York: Council of State Governments Justice Center, 2008.

Components laying the foundation of a reentry initiative, developing the initiative, implementing the plan, and making it stick are explained. The 10 elements of a comprehensive and effective reentry strategy are: viability; stakeholder involvement; initiative's priority population; mission, goals, and performance measures; initiative's terms and participant identification; information exchange and systems collaboration; transition planning; enhanced supervision; organizational capacity; and sustainability.

http://nicic.gov/Library/023295

Travis, Jeremy, et al. *Exploring the Role of the Police in Prisoner Reentry.* Cambridge, MA: Harvard Kennedy School, 2012.

"This paper is organized around two key elements. The first sets forth the basic parameters of the present-day reentry phenomenon in America, with a particular focus on two dimensions that intersect with the work of urban police departments: high recidivism rates and the concentration of returning prisoners in a few neighborhoods. The second explores two rationales for police involvement in prisoner reentry efforts: the promotion of public safety and the promotion of the legitimacy of the police" (p. 3). Sections of this publication cover: the realities of prisoner reentry in the United States—community concentrations, public safety and recidivism, and the national focus on prisoner reentry; reentry from county jails; prisoner reentry viewed through a policing lens—promoting public safety, and promoting police legitimacy; "East Palo Alto Police Department: A Case Study in Police Involvement in Prisoner Reentry"; and conclusion.

https://ncjrs.gov/pdffiles1/nij/238337.pdf

## REENTRY - SPECIAL POPULATIONS

Berman, Judith. *Women Offender Transition and Reentry: Gender Responsive Approaches to Transitioning Women Offenders from Prison to the Community.* Silver Spring, MD: Center for Effective Public Policy, 2005.

"This document summarizes the work on gender responsive approaches to women offenders in the context of the TPC [Transition from Prison to Community] Initiative, a system-wide approach to facilitating more effective transition of offenders from prison to the community" (p. 37). Sections comprising this report are: introduction; the need for gender responsiveness; women and transition -- assessment, behavior and programming, release preparation, release preparation; release, supervision and services, responses to violations, discharge, and aftercare; planning for a system-wide approach to transition; and conclusion. Appended are the diagrams "Critical Questions in Five Basic Life Areas at Key Decision Points of the TPC" and "Integrating Five Basic Life Areas of Women Offenders and Key Decision Points of the TPC."

http://nicic.gov/Library/021815

Bumby, Kurt, Tom Talbot, and Madeline Carter. *Managing the Challenges of Sex Offender Reentry.* Silver Spring, MD: Center for Sex Offender Management, 2007.

The "successful transition of sex offenders from prison to the community while ensuring victim and community safety" is explained (p.1). Sections of this policy and practice brief are: introduction; incarceration, release, and reincarceration trends with sex offenders; key elements of a sex offender reentry strategy; collaborate to achieve an "In to Out" approach; manage sex offenders in prison with an eye toward release; recognize the value of discretionary release decision making; to parole or not to parole sex offenders; "reach out" during the transition and release process; snapshot -- sex offender reentry in Vermont; snapshot -- using the Circles of Accountability and Support model to support sex offender reentry in Colorado; unintended consequences associated with community notification and residency restrictions; ensure victim-centeredness in the reentry process; adopt a success-oriented approach to post-release supervision; examples of dynamic risk factors relevant to post-release supervision and treatment of sex offenders; snapshot -- sex offender reentry in Texas; and conclusion.

http://www.csom.org/pubs/reentry_brief.pdf

*Critical Elements of Re-Entry/Continuing Care Systems [Participant's Manual].* Longmont, CO: National Institute of Corrections Academy, 2005.

"Using a three-phase process [during this 36-hour course] to plan, create, and evaluate reentry/continuing care systems, participant teams plan ways to help juvenile offenders from their jurisdictions successfully transition from institutional settings back into the community." Sections of this manual include: jurisdictional team action planning -- building your new reentry/continuing care reality; visualizing juvenile success in your reentry/continuing care jurisdiction; what are you currently bringing to the reentry/continuing care table?; becoming a change agent -- meeting the challenge; analyzing current practices -- discovering strengths and challenges; systems of care; and evaluation of reentry/continuing care.

http://nicic.gov/Library/020591

Cusick, Gretchen Ruth, Robert M. George, and Katie Claussen Bell. *From Corrections to Community: The Juvenile Reentry Experience as Characterized by Multiple Systems Involvement. Final report.* Chicago, IL: Illinois Criminal Justice Information Authority, 2008.

The impact of involvement in multiple systems on the recidivism of ex-offending juveniles in Illinois is investigated. Sections following an executive summary are: introduction; methods; findings -- description of systems involvement, profiles of multiple systems involvement in the collective reentry experience, and recidivism among youth with different reentry experiences; and discussion and implications. Involvement in multiple systems does not directly lead to lower recidivism rates.

http://nicic.gov/Library/023089

Daly, Reagan. *Treatment and Reentry Practices for Sex Offenders: An Overview of States*. New York: Vera Institute of Justice, 2008.

An "overview and analysis of existing treatment and reentry practices for sex offenders who are involved with the criminal justice system" is provided (p. iii). Sections following an executive summary include: introduction and background; methodology; research on prison- and community-based treatment, reentry programming, and community supervision; recent trends in prison- and community-based treatment, reentry programming, and community supervision; and conclusions. State overview tables for prison-based treatment, community-based treatment, reentry programming, and community supervision practices; and individual state templates.

http://nicic.gov/Library/023455

Greenberg, Richard. *Do No Harm: A Briefing Paper on the Reentry of Gang-Affiliated Individuals in New Jersey*. Newark, NJ: New Jersey Institute for Social Justice, 2007.

Strategies for reintegrating gang-affiliated offenders into New Jersey communities are explained. Sections after an executive summary are: introduction; background and context -- gangs and gang interventions, reentry dynamics of gang-affiliated individuals, and gang-related prison and parole programs in New Jersey; promising strategies -- pre-release and post-release interventions; and lessons learned.

http://www.njisj.org/documents/DoNoHarm_August2007_000.pdf

*Guidelines to Gang Reentry*. Lexington, KY: American Probation and Parole Association, 2011.

This guide provides suggestions "to assist gang-involved individuals returning to the community from confinement ... [and] for planning interventions for gang-involved defendants/offenders, along with helpful hints for facilitating effective and efficient reentry." Sections following the "Literature Review: Reentry and Gang-Affiliated Offenders" by James Howell are: institutional phase of reentry from intake to release; structured reentry phase—transitional work done by both the institution and community corrections; the community reintegration phase overseen by community corrections officers; and guiding principles for community reintegration.

http://nicic.gov/Library/024913

Lattimore, Pamela K., *et al. Prisoner Reentry Services: What Worked for SVORI Evaluation Participants? Final Report.* Washington, DC: National Institute of Justice, 2012.

Results from the second evaluation of the Serious and Violent Offender Reentry Initiative (SVORI), a large multi-site collection of state and local programs are presented. Sections of this report include: executive summary; introduction; current study—data and methods; subject characteristics; results for adult males and for adult females according to housing, employment, victimization, compliance with supervision requirements, drug use, recidivism, summary and discussion; results for juvenile males by housing, employment, victimization, drug use, and recidivism; economic evaluation for adult males; and discussion and policy implications. "The effect of SVORI program participation was beneficial and statistically significant for all three demographic groups – associated with longer times to arrest and with fewer arrests during fixed follow-up periods. Results were weaker for the effects of SVORI on post-release reincarceration" (p. ES-5).

http://nicic.gov/Library/026076

Lowe, Nathan C., and Matthew DeMichele. *Reentry of Methamphetamine-Using Offenders into the Community: Identifying Key Strategies and Best Practices for Community Corrections.* Lexington, KY: American Probation and Parole Association, 2010.

If you or your agency is reintegrating ex-offenders that used methamphetamines (MA) into the community, you own it to yourselves to read this publication. "The purpose of this report is to highlight the need for a coherent strategy for community corrections professionals to use when supervising MA-using populations in the community. This report offers the community corrections field baseline data to understand some of the obstacles and lessons learned regarding supervision of MA-using offenders" (p. 1). This information comes from a focus group and three technical assistance sites in Colorado, South Dakota, and Arizona. Results from the focus group cover treatment, sentencing and sanctions, supervision, collaboration, and public safety concerns. The technical assistance sites yielded information regarding 14 best practices, some of which are: the establishment of local interagency committees; more effective lines of communication between community supervising officers; and better access to support services.

http://nicic.gov/Library/025734

Lowman, Jennifer, and Shari A. Mamas. *Educational Aftercare & Reintegration Toolkit for Juvenile Justice Professionals: A Toolkit for Juvenile Justice Professionals in Pennsylvania.* 2nd ed. Philadelphia, PA: Models for Change Education Law Center, 2009.

This toolkit is designed to "serve as a roadmap for identifying issues related to the education of delinquent youth during placement and when they are released and reintegrated into their communities" (p. 7). Nine sections are contained in this toolkit: introduction; pre-placement dispositional hearing; educational services in placement; release and reintegration into the community; enrollment, attendance, and truancy; special education and other in-school services; school discipline; where to go for more help and information; and conclusion. Included are Checklist of Key Activities from Pre-Placement through Release and Reintegration" and samples of 18 specific tools for use in juvenile offender aftercare and reintegration.

http://nicic.gov/Library/023952

Prendergast, Michael L. *Interventions to Promote Successful Re-Entry among Drug-Abusing Parolees [and] Response: Pathways to Recovery and Reintegration.* Bethesda, MD: National Institute on Drug Abuse, 2009.

Reviews research findings on principles of effective correctional treatment and the interventions that have been shown to be effective with drug abusing parolees or that have been tested with general drug-abusing populations and shown promise for use with parolees.

http://nicic.gov/Library/024158

Reichert, Jessica, Dawn Ruzich, and Rebecca Campbell. *Community Reentry after Prison Drug Treatment: Learning from Sheridan Therapeutic Community Program Participants.* Chicago, IL: Illinois Criminal Justice Information Authority, 2012.

Results from an evaluation of the Sheridan Correctional Center National Drug Prison and Reentry Program are provided. Graduates remained two years in the community before re-incarceration, on average.

http://nicic.gov/Library/025653

*Strategies for Creating Offender Reentry Programs in Indian Country.* Albuquerque, NM: American Indian Development Associates, 2010.

"The information presented in this document will assist tribal justice practitioners, administrators, and policymakers in designing and developing reentry strategies for adult and juvenile offenders returning to their tribal communities" (p. 5). Sections of this report include: introduction; historical overview; developing reentry programs in Indian Country—justice system, intervention and treatment, and community restoration; general reentry policy considerations—Tribal government responsibilities, funding, and Tribal community roles; recommendations; conclusion; case descriptions; and federal funding sources.

http://nicic.gov/Library/024788

*Women Offender Case Management Model.* Ottawa, ON: Orbis Partners, Inc., 2006.

The gender-responsive Women Offender Case Management Model (WOCMM) is described. This document covers: the history of the project; philosophy and core practices; process incorporating four core elements (e.g., engage and assess, enhance motivation, implement the case plan, and review progress); preparing for implementation; and evaluation.

http://nicic.gov/Library/021814

Zarch, Rebecca. *A Practitioner's "Blueprint" for Replication.* Cambridge, MA: Abt Associates, 2007.

Designed to share the lessons learned from Women Offender Reentry Collaborative, including organizations that are already serving similar populations and those considering expanding or modifying services.

http://www.doleta.gov/pri/pdf/WORC_Blueprint_7_12.pdf

Zimmermann, Carol Rapp, Gina Hendrix, James Moeser, and David W. Roush, eds. *Desktop Guide to Reentry for Juvenile Confinement Facilities.* East Lansing MI: Center for Research & Professional Development, National Juvenile Detention Association, July 2004.

Components of an effective juvenile reentry process are described. Sections of this guide include: the roots of reentry—what we can learn from history, research, and theory; equipping for reentry success—building partnerships, coalitions, and independence; reinventing the process—shifting to a reentry mission, case plan, and transition plan; defining reentry for short-term stays; data to drive decisions--measuring reentry success; marketing reentry--agenda setting and the media; summary of risk and protective factors by domain; Texas Youth Commission Service Department Independent Living Subsidy Program Contract and Conditions of Placement; defining roles from confinement to community; Planning for Transition--the Massachusetts Department of Youth Services' Model; the tasks of community reentry--what institutions do; and the Santa Cruz County Juvenile Detention Screening Risk Assessment.

http://wccf.org/pdf/REENTRY%20-%20DESKTOP%20GUIDE%20TO%20JUV%20OFFENDER%20REENTRY.pdf

## REENTRY SKILLS BUILDING

*2012 Reentry Skills Building Handbook.* Forsyth, GA: Georgia Department of Corrections, 2012.

While the local services are Georgia based, the bulk of this handbook contains a wealth of excellent information and resources that will help an ex-offender make a successful transition back into the community. Forms and checklists for the released individual to fill out are spread throughout this guide and make the reentry process less intimidating. Not only giving the ex-offender direction, this handbook can be used by the community corrections practitioner in making sure the reentry process is effective for the ex-offender. Chapters following an introduction about getting organized cover identification, housing, employment, careers, work ethics, transportation, money management, education, applying for social security, health and life skills, mental health, alcohol and other drugs (AOD) and recovery, family and friend relationships, child support, and living under supervision.

http://nicic.gov/Library/026067

*Adult Pre-Release Handbook: Pre-Release Information for an Informed Re-Entry and a Successful Transition.* 5<sup>th</sup> ed. St. Paul: Minnesota Department of Corrections, 2010.

This guide will help offenders in determining where they are at in terms of preparing for release and in creating a plan to succeed once they leave prison. This handbook contains eleven chapters: identification; life skills; housing; education; transportation; living under supervision; family; restorative justice; health; money management; and employment.

http://nicic.gov/Library/024755

Atkinson, Rhonda, *et al. Project Metamorphosis.* Baton Rouge, LA: Louisiana Dept. of Public Safety and Corrections, 1999.

Project Metamorphosis was created to enhance the education and training of adult inmates in order to reduce recidivism. A functionally-contextual educational curriculum was developed integrating basic academic, employability, and cognitive skills training for learners at a variety of skill levels. The newsletter format is utilized within this curriculum because it is appropriate for adult learners and easily duplicated. This website provides access to the eight volumes of this program. Titles of the volumes are: Learning About Project Metamorphosis and self; Success is a Thinking Skill -- Work; Keys to Loving Relationships; Success is a Thinking Skill -- Decision-Making; Keys to Loving Relationships [part 2]; Finding and Keeping Jobs; Parenting Series; and Money Management.

http://www.learningconnections.org/going_home/meta.htm

Bush, Jack, Barry Glick, and Juliana Taymans. *Thinking for a Change: Integrated Cognitive Behavior Change Program.* Version 3.1. Washington, DC: National Institute of Corrections, 2011.

Thinking for a Change (T4C) is an integrated, cognitive behavior change program for offenders that includes cognitive restructuring, social skills development, and development of problem solving skills. T4C is designed for delivery to small groups in 25 lessons and can be expanded on to meet the needs of specific participant group. The T4C program is used in prisons, jails, community corrections, probation, and parole supervision settings. Participants include adults and juveniles, males and females.

http://nicic.gov/Library/025057

*Career Resource Centers: An Emerging Strategy for Improving Offender Employment Outcomes.* Washington, DC: National Institute of Corrections, 2010.

"This bulletin highlights the ways career resource centers are being used in jails, prisons, and community supervision offices to improve the long-term employment prospects of offenders" (p.1). Sections of this publication include: common elements of career resource centers; getting started; working with inmate career clerks; building community ties; role of assessment in career resource centers; technology resources; finding champions and overcoming resistance; and future directions. The following resources are contained on the DVD: a PDF version of the bulletin; video interviews with many of the practitioners features in the bulletin; the CareerZone program; reentry guides from federal, state, and local correctional facilities; the Veterans Incarcerated Employability Workshop; a life-skills curriculum; virtual tours of career resource centers; links to Internet resources that promote the development of career resource centers; and career development documents that can be distributed to the inmate population.

http://nicic.gov/Library/023066

Cox, Brian A., Judy Burd, and Ed Roberts. *Cognitive Intervention: A Program for Offenders, WSD's TurningPoint.* Rev. [ed.] Huntsville, TX: Texas Dept. of Criminal Justice Windham School District, 1997.

WSD's Turning Point Program is an instructional curriculum designed to help offenders overcome criminal thinking and behavior and to reduce the recidivism of offenders through cognitive restructuring and cognitive skill development. This document contains a Facilitator's Manual, which includes such topics as motivating self-change in offenders, promoting change in a group setting, class climate, guidelines for managing classroom behavior, and thinking reports, and a Curriculum Manual that consists of 16 lessons with accompanying handouts. Lesson topics include: criminal addictive cycle, problem solving, thinking errors, choices and consequences, time management skills, and relapse prevention. Also provided is WSD's relapse prevention booklet and a copy of the Criminal Sentiments Scale developed by Don Andrews and Steve Wormith. The earlier DETOUR curriculum is embedded within this document.

*Employment Information Handbook.* Washington, DC: U.S. Bureau of Prisons 2011.

This handbook "provides prisoners with contacts and other information that can help them to prepare for release" (p. 2). Sections contained in this guide are: purpose; what to do to prepare for release; employers who hire ex-offenders; federal programs to help ex-offenders; state and federal jobs for ex-offenders; loans and grants; programs sponsored by the U.S. Department of Labor; other programs not directly related to employment; how to get a birth certificate; state contacts for vital documents; how to get a driver's license; state contacts for driver license information; Veterans Vocational Rehabilitation and Employment Service; how to get money to continue ones education; and appendixes—job search information, sample resume, sample job application, and Federal Bonding Program State Bonding Coordinators.

http://nicic.gov/Library/024941

*Fair Shake Reentry Resource Center: Tools for a Successful Transition.* Fair Shake, 2012.

A wealth of information about how an ex-offender can transition successfully into the community can be found at this website. "Fair Shake is dedicated to reducing the recidivism rate through personal and community focused ownership and engagement opportunities for inmates and former felons in connection with families, employers, property managers, and corrections." Points of entry include: Resource Directory; Reentry Toolkit; Information Center; about Fair Shake; getting involved; and Member Area.

http://www.fairshake.net/index.html

*The Maryland Prison to Work Project: Facilitator's Resource Handbook.* Baltimore: Maryland State Department of Education, 2001.

"[I]nformation, curriculum and activities ...proven to be effective with preparing offenders for release, transition, and employment" are provided (p. I-4). The following sections comprise this manual: introduction; course narrative; instructional and career resources–overview, resource list, "The Art of Facilitation," career readiness handouts covering assessments, general employment information, vital records and employment laws and regulations, career exploration and job search, applications, cover letters and resumes, and interviewing, and instructional activities regarding assessment, exploration, job search, and transition/employment; career center; job fairs; and transition and retention services.

http://www.msde.state.md.us/prisontowork/index.html

*Prisoner Reentry Resource Manual.* Anchorage: Alaska Department of Corrections, 2010.

The Reentry Manual includes nine Steps to successful reentry, and is designed to function as both a teacher's guide and inmate workbook, with space to take notes, checklists to gauge reentry readiness and worksheets to create resumes, budgets and spending logs. Objectives are listed at the beginning of each Step, followed by a simple, step by step process for meeting them.

http://www.correct.state.ak.us

Ransom, Gary R., and Scott Nicholson. *Offender Transition Program: Resource Manual.* Washington, DC: U. S. Bureau of Prisons, 2010.

Information for inmates making the transition back into the community is provided in this manual. Resources are organized into the following sections: Internet resources; career exploration; general assistance programs; business/consumer education; substance abuse and mental health; and appendixes covering the Department of Labor state level contacts, U.S. Department of Housing and Urban Development, U.S. Small Business

Administration, Service Corp of Retired Executives, and the Federal Reserve Bank.

http://nicic.gov/Library/024942

*Reasoning Skills Program [Lesson Plan].* Fairfield, IA: Department of Correctional Services, 2005.

Access to the Reasoning Skills Program for offenders on probation is provided. This set of 12 lessons "are designed to help you learn to think more clearly and to show you how to make decisions that get you what you want without creating new problems for yourself or others" (p. 1). Lessons cover: what does it mean to have a problem; responses are not an accident; bicameral mind (emotional and rational decisions); values; management of emotions; Darth Vader versus Robert E. Lee (understanding the dangers of being seduced by the emotions of power, control, and elation); problem solving; fate, nature, and nurture (the negative consequences associated with blaming these for ones problems); callous heart; Insurance Game (to show how the harm done by a criminal act goes far beyond the act itself); Isaiah (that being part of a system contributes its negative consequences even if one does not directly participate in the wrong themselves); and finding your way (life goals).

http://www.8thjdcbc.com/VirtualClassroom.htm

*Reentry Readiness Manual.* New Brunswick, NJ: Rutgers University, 2008

This assessment of ten questions, is an effective way to see whether the offender feels s/he is ready to successfully reenter the community.

http://www.cbhs-cjr.rutgers.edu/pdfs/REENTRY_Assessment_final_ doc.pdf

*Simulated Online/Kiosk Job Application.* Washington, DC: National Institute of Corrections, 2008.

Each year, more and more employers are requiring job applicants to apply online or at a computer kiosk. Offenders in prisons, jails, parole and probation offices, faith-based agencies, and community-based organizations can use this CD-ROM to practice completing an employment application using a computer that does not have access to the Internet. This simulation training program provides basic information about computerized employment applications, tips for completing online job applications, a printable worksheet that can be used to prepare offenders for using these systems, and a full-length interactive application with context sensitive help. At the completion of the process, the user can print out the information that was entered.

http://nicic.gov/Library/022996

# End Notes

[1] Sabol, W. & H.C. West. *Prisoners in 2009*. NCJ 231675. Washington, D.C.: U.S. Department of Justice, Bureau of Justice Statistics, 2010. bjs.ojp.usdoj.gov/content/pub/pdf/p09.pdf.

[2] Beck, A.J. *The Importance of Successful Reentry to Jail Population Growth.* Presented at the Urban Institute's Jail Reentry Roundtable, June 27, 2006. www.urban.org/projects/reentry-roundtable/upload/beck.PPT.

[3] Langan, P.A. & D.J. Levin. *Recidivism of Prisoners Released in 1994*. NCJ 193427. Washington, D.C.: U.S. Department of Justice, Bureau of Justice Statistics, 2002. bjs.ojp. usdoj.gov/content/pub/pdf/rpr94.pdf

[4] Pew Center on the States, One in 31: The Long Reach of American Corrections (Washington, DC: The Pew Charitable Trusts, March 2009).

# INDEX